# AND IT
# BEGINS
# LIKE
# THIS

# AND IT BEGINS LIKE THIS

LaTanya McQueen

Black
Lawrence
Press

Black
Lawrence
Press

www.blacklawrence.com

Executive Editor: Diane Goettel
Book and Cover Design: Amy Freels

Copyright © LaTanya McQueen 2018
ISBN: 978-1-62557-703-0

Published 2018 by Black Lawrence Press.
Printed in the United States.

*For those who have yet to be seen,*
*and for those who have yet to be heard.*

# Contents

# In the Name of the Fathers

In Caswell County, North Carolina if one were to drive down U.S. Route 158, you'd come to the intersection of U.S. Route 150. Turn right on 150, and a little ways on you'll see a placard for Bedford Brown:

> *Bedford Brown, U.S. Senator, 1829–30, State Legislator,*
> *Opponent of Secession, 1860.*
> *This is "Rose Hill." His Home.*

The placard seems easy to miss if you're not looking for it. It's not often one pays attention to the signs of history, and in the summer when the wind sways it could be partially obscured by the trees. Past this placard and on down a road you can barely see you'd eventually find Brown's plantation home, known colloquially as the Bedford Brown House. In 1973 it was listed in the National Register of Historic Places, but it's a private residence now so there are no tours. Without context the house looks unremarkable. From photos, it is a two-story Colonial style house, the exterior painted white with dark green shutters. Thick rose bushes frame the front. If you're there in the summer, one can imagine the smell of wild roses filling the air.

Near this plantation, hidden among the looming cedar trees, is a small unpaved road, a path really, once known to my family as Siddle Road, and it is here at this crossing where the origins of my family history begins.

Let's start with what I know.

My grandfather's name was Marvin Siddle. He was the second youngest of twelve children. One of Marvin's older brothers, William, bore the same name of his father—William Lovelace Siddle, listed also as Wells on the 1920 census. This is confusing until I remember how notoriously inaccurate census records were. "What's your husband's name?" I imagine the census taker asking, his throat scratchy from thirst, as he stood on the front stoop of yet another farm. "I can't hear you. Say it again? Well?"

So Well L. Siddle, nicknamed sometimes Billie by his family, formally called William (named after his father), who is listed as mulatto on this census.

This is what I know.

I also know that there is an earlier 1880 census for a William Siddle, also married, but this one—this one listed as white.

"We should have been Browns," my godmother tells me. She is also my mother's cousin. They grew up on neighboring farms and worked the tobacco fields together. Despite this parallel, once the evening came my godmother would venture home to schoolwork whereas my mother continued working the fields far late into the night. There's guilt in her voice when we talk of the past and I've often wondered how much of their upbringing factored into what their lives would become. It's a question I sense she's thought about as well but I dare not ever ask.

"The census may say Siddle," she explains, "but it should have been Brown, had the mother named the children after her slave name, but she didn't. They have the surname of another man, a white one."

The woman my godmother is talking about is Leanna Brown, my great-great-grandmother. Leanna Brown, nicknamed by her children as Granny Brown, once a slave of the Bedford Browns.

The folklore in my family has always been that Leanna "had 'em up" or took William Siddle, the father of her children, to court to make sure they carried his name. This would have been during the height of Reconstruction, before Jim Crow took its fierce hold of the South.

"I never believed my father when he told me the story. I always thought he made it up, but I've learned through research that during that time plenty of women did something similar. So while I didn't believe him before I believe him now," she said.

It took my mother's death to make me question the pieces of her life and the person I knew. I've begun to reexamine what could have been possible as explanation for the way she was.

Tell me though, how does one begin to find the truth in the past? Who do you turn to when most of the people who could have known are gone?

If a given name can be a marker of a cultural identity then my name is marked as black. I knew this as a child. I told myself what I hated was the pause of uncertainty on the first day of class when a teacher did roll. "Laa—" they'd begin, the uncertainty in their voice. "Just tell me what it is," finally saying as they sighed with resignation.

I hated also the misspellings that inevitably happened. The sheer unwillingness to learn, instead writing their own versions of a signifier of my identity.

These were the reasons I used as justification when I asked my mother if I could have my name changed. Deep down, my mother had always resented my name as well. Perhaps it was because my father might have mistakenly told her the story of why he picked it. ("I knew a girl with that name and I thought she was the hottest thing I ever saw!") Or it could be because of the simple fact that my father gave it to me. At the time they were in the midst of a divorce and she could have used this as a tactic of revenge. I suspect though that her reasons were the same ones I'd finally admit to myself that I also had. She hated the names associations—that I am black, that before anyone knew me they would know my name and what it signified.

My father, for obvious reasons, would not agree to the decision to change my name. "Why don't you want your name?" he would say over and over to a crying child on the phone. "Why don't you want to be who you are?"

What I am interested in now are the ways in which a series of circumstances and actions can contribute to the people we become.

"Be glad you're not dark," I remember my mother telling me as a child. "Be glad you have light skin and good hair that doesn't kink up too much. People will like you more. Not too much, because you're still black, but more."

I will think of my mother's words often throughout my life. They will help to explain the reasons for why as a child I will scrub my skin raw, ashamed even then of my blackness. I'll think of them when, like with my name, I'll seek to change other parts of myself. My hair will grow out long. I'll wear blue contact lenses. The combination of these making acquaintances and friends question. "What are you?" they'll ask, reaching out for the briefest of seconds to touch my hair.

And I'll lie when people ask me my race. They'll always ask and I'll tell them I am mixed. I'll say whatever I think I can get away with. "Which one of your parents is white?" they'll always assume, and this will be where I always falter, wondering which one of my parents to erase.

My mother grew up on a farm in a place called Ruffin, North Carolina. Ruffin is less than thirteen miles away from the Locust Hill Township in Caswell County. Locust Hill, specifically an area called Rose Hill, is where the original Siddle farm was located.

The story here is that there were two plantations. The first belonging to the Bedford Browns and nearby, down a path, a smaller plantation of a white family named Siddles. A man named Will Siddle had a relationship with Leanna Brown, a slave or servant of the Bedford Browns.

Their relationship produced three children, one being my great-grandfather William, sometimes called Billie, Siddle. Some time when Billie is older he'll get enough money together to buy land and build that house in Ruffin. That house will be the one my grandfather will grow up in and eventually my mother will too.

I've tried, many times, to fully render in my mind the image of that house. It was white, two floors, with a black roof. No indoor plumbing, at least not while my mother is growing up, and she'll tell me about her late night ventures in the dark to the outhouse. She'll talk about her fear of snakes reaching up from the hole. The smell.

Open the front door and you're in the living room. Adjacent to this and separated by two large French doors is the kitchen. In my mind, I'll convince myself I remember these doors but really what I'm remembering is the telling of the doors to me throughout the years. A hallway leads to a staircase where if one were to walk up they'd be taken to one of the three bedrooms. Downstairs are where the other two bedrooms are—my mother's, which she shared with her brother, and her parents'. Further down the hallway is the kitchen where there's another door leading out back.

None of this is of particular interest except for one detail: a door is affixed to the entryway leading upstairs. This door will be locked. No one except for Mayo, my great-uncle, who lives with the rest of the family, will ever be allowed to go up there.

Let me rephrase that—it is not "no one except for my great-uncle will be allowed up there" but rather my great-uncle will not be allowed in the rest of the house. The locked door, I'm told, is not to prevent the rest of the family from interacting with him, but to prevent him from the rest of the family.

"Mayo?" On the phone, my grandmother pauses to think. I'd been looking through census records when I stopped at this name, not recognizing it. "Oh yeah. We called him Pigaboy—Pigger sometimes. It was always that. Not Mayo."

"Pigger?" I ask, not going further. My grandmother does not like to talk about the family of the husband she was once married to. It's been decades since his death, but my grandmother still flinches when I ask about him or his relatives. There is the sense she was not treated well by them. Even though she'll never tell me, my father will relay stories of how she was beaten by her husband and how his brothers and sisters disregarded her because her skin was not light like theirs.

Most of them were light-skinned, some bordering on even looking white. If you saw a picture you'd think they were Italian maybe, or Jewish, and they could have passed if they wanted.

It bears mentioning that like my grandmother, Mayo was darker too.

"Yeah, because he ate like a pig," my grandmother says. "He ate his food like a dark little pig, you know Pigger. Pigaboy."

"You know what Pigger sounds an awful lot like," I say to her, thinking of all this.

"Yes, well," my grandmother responds. She swallows hard in the phone. "I realize this now."

Mayo, born 1920, and sometimes called Pigaboy or Pigger by his family.

As I've mentioned, Mayo will live upstairs. The downstairs door that leads to the rest of the house will be locked from him. His only route of access will be to the door out back. His meals will be placed on the back porch where he'll either eat them or carry them back upstairs.

There are reasons for all this. Mayo eats like a pig so his nickname will be Pigaboy, shortened to Pigger. My family will say he's unstable, explaining that there were been incidents but never explicitly telling me what they were. To keep the rest of the family safe, especially the children, the doors had to be locked. Mayo couldn't be with everyone else, he had to be separated. He had to eat his food out back. It was all they knew what to do. It was the only way.

Mayo's death record shows that he died on January 17, 1973 at the age of fifty-two. What it doesn't show is that he died upstairs in his bedroom and that it will be days before the rest of the family notices.

"Down in Yanceyville Billie went as white," my godmother tells me. "That's what I've always heard, and remember it was eight miles to Yanceyville from Caswell and this was horse and buggies time, you actually had to travel to get there. So why would the people there think that this man was white? Under what circumstances would they imagine that to be the case? The only reason I can think of is because he went there to see his father, and if he's with his father out in public that means his father must have claimed him—not only claiming but helping him, and in light of all that it fits in to the paradigm that the relationship his father had with him was consensual."

There is a slight pause. Before I'm able to respond she continues again.

"Also, in the consensual relationships I've read about, the child bears the name of the father."

In *The Fluidity of Race: "Passing" in the United States, 1880-1940*, Emily Nix and Nancy Qian estimate that "using the full population of historical Censuses from 1880-1940, we document that over 19% of black males 'passed' for white at some point during their lifetime."

Billie Siddle, my great-grandfather, will periodically pass for white. I'll hear versions of this from my mother as well, but she'll explain he left to pass and work the coal mines in Virginia, making enough money to come back and buy the land and build his own farm the family will live on decades later.

If Billie could pass, and if in fact there were circumstances when he did, then what made him decide not to?

Maybe the answer to this question is the behind the reason he'll have issues with skin color the rest of his life. He'll pass them on to his children, each of them harboring the same prejudices, and they'll pass them on to their children—to my mother and eventually to me.

Billie Siddle will die on November 11, 1923, at the age of 48. The cause of death being chronic nephritis, a disease caused by infections, most commonly caused by autoimmune disorders that affect the organs, like lupus, a disease my mother will come to suffer from.

On the death certificate, in the space for the name of the father, there is only a question mark.

In the story of Cain and Abel from the book of Genesis, Eve bears two sons—Cain, a tiller of the earth, and Abel, a shepherd. When they both offer sacrifices to God, Abel's is respected more, much to the jealousy of Cain. Acting out of his own anger, he takes Abel into a field and kills him, and when God asks him where Abel is, he answers, "I know not, am I my brother's keeper?"

After God finds out the truth about Abel's murder, he curses Cain for what he's done. Cain pleads with God, explaining that this punishment is too much for him to bear. If he is a fugitive and a vagabond, then anyone who happens to find him will kill him. Hearing this, God tells him that whoever slays him will have vengeance taken upon them sevenfold. "And the Lord set a mark upon Cain, lest any finding him should kill him."

Theologians have interpreted this mark in many different ways. Some believe it to be a symbol of God's promise of protection. Others have suggested that the mark was a distinguishing characteristic God gave so that people would see and not harm him. In the 18th century it was taught that the Cain's mark was black skin and that his descendants were black and still under the "the curse of Cain."

There is no clear consensus as to which of these definitions is being referred to regarding Cain's mark.

In the famous Clark doll experiments conducted in the 1940s, husband and wife team Kenneth and Mamie Clark gave a child two different dolls, identical except for their skin color and hair. One doll was white with yellow hair and the other doll was brown with black hair. Then, the child was asked questions like "Which is the pretty doll?" "Which is the bad doll?"

Of course, you know this story already, even what the answers were, that their findings showed the internalized racism present among the children, the majority of which showed a preference for the white doll.

In 2006, Kiri Davis recreated the experiment for her documentary *A Girl Like Me*. Davis found that, nearly seventy years later, nothing much had changed. Girls still picked the white doll. The pretty doll. The good doll.

I do not need to wonder which doll I would have picked had I been asked. Growing up, I never had black dolls. The choice for me was never even a possibility.

*Seeking information on the mixed or african american siddle family. Possible starting with a Billie Siddle. —Kim*

A message posted on a genealogy forum. The date January 15, 2002.

I'm able to send to a response to the original poster. *Hi Kim, I believe I am someone you're looking for. Please write me back.*

No one will answer.

Unlike with Billie, there is next to nothing on Leanna Brown. She was married but I'm unsure of the dates. If she was a slave then it's possible her marriage would not have been recorded.

In search of answers I decide to look through the cohabitation records for the county. If I'm able to document when she was married then perhaps it will clarify the nature of her relationship with William Siddle. It could potentially offer clues to who the other children were.

Cohabitation records were created to legitimize marriages and children born to those in slavery. In these records, the information can include names of the individuals, ages, places where they were born, the names of their last known slave holders, and approximate year of marriage or cohabitation. These records can often be found in local courthouses, state archives, and libraries.

I check the website of the North Carolina State Archives and it says that cohabitation records are known to have survived for the following counties, but Caswell County is not included in this list.

Once, in graduate school I fell in love with a white boy who was unaware of my feelings. One night we were in a Starbucks talking. The cashier had begun her closing up ritual but we continued to stay.

I showed him an article about a celebrity who'd recently made some racist comments regarding his own dating preferences. I mentioned it off the cuff even though there was more to be said—a larger conversation about racial bias and prejudices in dating preferences, for one thing, or the effects of European beauty standards on women of color, or even the current problems in interracial dating. There was more to be interrogated between us but the minutes were quickly ticking by and soon we were the only customers left.

"That's some bullshit," he responded. "Who does this guy think he is?"

His anger, far worse than mine, made me believe he was trying to tell me something more, but then I remembered this was all a surprise to him. He had no idea what it was like to experience these attitudes day in and out. He was a conventionally attractive male with parents who would have given him the world. His anger came from a place where injustice was never a reality.

In the end, nothing ever happened between us. He fell in love with someone else. Her skin the color of cream.

On her Facebook page I find a photo of the two of them. Many times there will be moments when my thoughts will get the best of me and I'll go back to that photo and wonder if the reason nothing ever happened between us was because I did not look the way he was wanting.

Before the death of my mother I was not a person who talked about race. I was a person who actively avoided it throughout most of my life. It was easy when you were the only black person in a room, when for years you were the only black person you know. You find ways to adapt to the world around you, joining in with all the appropriate cultural signifiers, and because my skin was light enough I thought somehow I would be enough, that I'd be accepted beyond the Other that I am.

My desire to fit these pieces I have in a certain way is strong, undeniable, but I find myself asking what to make of them. How does one begin to compile these bits of fact, these stories and anecdotes, together into a way of understanding?

I struggle to turn them into a narrative that makes sense, so all I can do is offer them in the hope that somewhere one can find the truth.

According to population projections by the U.S. Census Bureau, by the year 2044 whites will become the minority. There will be a growth of new minorities, from Asians, Hispanics, and those identifying as multiracial. This last group—multiracials—will more than triple in number.

The same day I read this in the news I find an article about the rise of ethnic plastic surgeries cropping up in the U.S. Rhinoplasties to sharpen the flat shape of an ethnic-looking nose, for example, or "facial contouring" procedures in which the bones of the jaw are cut to make the appearance a v-shape.

"I think we're kind of losing ethnic niches. I don't think there's going to be a black race or a white race or an Asian race," Dr. Michael Jones, a plastic surgeon, is quoted saying in the article. "Essentially, in 200 years, we're going to have one race."

On my teaching evaluations my students say I discuss race too much. They are angry because in talking about American literature, I force them to read Charles W. Chesnutt, the first African American fiction writer. We read the slave narratives of Harriet Jacobs and Frederick Douglass. We read W.E.B. Du Bois and Booker T. Washington. I bring in recordings of the Harlem Renaissance poets and let them hear the music and rhythm in Langston Hughes's "The Negro Speaks of Rivers." They listen to the songs of Negro spirituals. I bring in Toni Morrison and Amiri Baraka, and I make them read James Baldwin's "Going to Meet the Man," a story that makes my hands shake every time I read it. That day, I spend an hour in front of my mostly white class talking about the Klan. I show them pictures of lynchings, one after the other after the other. I tell them of the brutal, ugly history of our country so that they can try to understand the world Baldwin has come from, but they never do.

The day I teach Baldwin everyone is bracing to hear the decision about Michael Brown and so the first thing I do is take a piece of chalk and begin writing. On the board I write the names I've collected of the black men and women throughout history who've been murdered—whether lynched or shot by police. One by one I write their names, filling the board with my scrawled script.

I leave it up during the remainder of the class, and towards the end, when I feel my own energy draining, I tell him that it's important to remember. "There is a pattern," I say, repeating the theory my godmother once told me. She believes that in looking at history, in seeing the moments of racial progress for African Americans there has always been a steep backlash in response. It happened after the Civil War with the creation of the KKK, it happened after Reconstruction with the rise of the Jim Crow era in the South, and it happened after the Civil Rights Movement with the KKK's reemergence.

"Recognize it and maybe you can change it, because the problem is we keep forgetting."

Then I erase the board, slowly, hoping with this action the point hits home, but they are already packing their bags and out the door.

"I used to see Leanna as a victim," my godmother tells me. "She was in the sense that she was a black woman and didn't have any power, but the more I delve into the past, the more I've come to fully understand how much people don't fit into the boxes history wants us to put them in."

I've wanted to believe that the basis of their relationship was love, that Leanna Brown took the name for her children because she wanted a piece of this man to hold onto, to be carried down among the generations. It is a story that goes down better than what history is known to provide—that her children were the product of rape.

I'm not sure how much I believe in generational curses, if the sins of the fathers shall be passed on to the children and then to their children's children.

Yet the patterns in my family are certainly there, repeating among generation to generation, and so for me the name carries with it a mark, a stain. It is more than the mark of my race, with that name are years of self-hatred, of anger, of wrongs done I can barely fathom and will never fully understand.

So how then can a name that carries so much pain with it have come from love?

Of course though, my students are unaware about race. To them I am just a black teacher talking about race when they don't want to talk about race. They are unaware of the history that has come to define my existence.

*"Don't you understand?"* I want to explain. *"Do you even understand how long it's taken me to get here? To get to this point of even the acknowledgement of who I am?"*

I'm in a bar sitting alone. A man comes up and sits down next to me. "Grading, I see?" he interrupts, nodding toward my stack of papers, and for a moment I am willing to go along, to be distracted.

"Yes."

"I want to ask——" and here it comes. I know the question before he even finishes, but he is looking at me and whatever expression on my face makes him stop. Instead, he tries a different tactic and softly mutters Spanish.

"What?"

"Oh," he says, realizing his mistake, but the question is there and he still must know the answer. "I thought you were maybe one of my Dominican sisters? I've been hoping to find some of my people here in this town."

"I'm sorry," I say, then pick up another paper.

"So you're not?" he continues, not taking the hint. "I mean, *you're* not?"

"I'm black."

"Really?" He draws the word out so it sounds more like an accusation than a question.

"Yes."

This is the part where I'm supposed to offer up evidence. I'm supposed to explain how both of my parents were light-skinned, or mention how I have my mother's curls. I'll explain how I have great aunts and uncles who passed, and the colorism issues most of us face, but by then I'll have gone on too long. I'll have said too much. What will be wanted is an explanation, not an indictment or a history lesson on racial constructions.

This time though I say nothing. I reach for my wallet and take out a twenty, placing it on the counter. I grab my stack of papers and stand, leaving the bar and the man with just my simple answer, my affirmation—yes.

This time it is enough.

I spend my time now going through the Civil Action Court Records of North Carolina. They are searchable online. In this collection, spanning from 1709 to 1970, are records consisting of civil disputes pertaining to land ownership, unpaid debts, slave manumissions, divorces, and the legitimization of children born out of wedlock.

Somewhere buried in these pages of pages of documents I feel as if I'll find my answer. If ever there was a place to look this is it—the answer to the name and how it came to be in my family.

Because I do not have a specific date to go by there are thousands of pages I must search. There are so many names. Some of the documents are faded and it's difficult to see. My eyes squint trying to make out the cursive.

There is a chance I will go through all these and find nothing. Perhaps there was never anything to find.

Yet, I am here. At night when the world has quieted, I sit at my desk, coffee in hand. Each scan takes a few seconds to load and I wait and sip. Names flash across my screen—names of strangers, of brothers and sisters bonded together, of mothers and daughters, of fathers and sons, names of the searching, names of the lost, names waiting for someone who will one day find and claim them.

# Before You Throw Her Body Down

In the bar's bathroom I stand in front of the mirror and rub my lips together, pressing hard, smearing the color I've just applied. The color is a blueish red, a date-night color, from a tube of lipstick I've bought but never worn.

Tonight, I am here to meet a man. Some of his friends and some of my friends who know each other have suggested we meet. Partly, I suspect, because we are both black, and we are both single, and for them that is enough of a reason for why we should be together.

He is out there somewhere now, possibly already at the bar, possibly already searching among the other patrons for who I might be. Or he is standing outside waiting in the cold, the puffs of his breath dissipating as he looks up and down the streets watching to see who else comes to the door. He is out there and I am in this bathroom fooling with a color, and as I look at my reflection it is the only color I see.

Another woman comes inside and the disruption makes me blush. Quickly, I take a tissue from my bag, wet it, and wipe the lipstick off, the smear on the tissue a reminder. I wipe until there is nothing but the blank canvas of my mouth and then I leave to find the man I'm supposed to meet.

There is a story I must tell you and it begins like this—once, a woman once had a relationship with a man. Her name was a Leanna Brown and she was a slave to Bedford Brown and his family. Bedford Brown was Senator of North Carolina during the 1830s. Next to Brown's plantation lived a man by the name of William Siddle. The two of them, Leanna and William, sometimes called Willie, had a relationship that resulted in at least two, possibly three children, and one of those children was my great-grandfather.

When I look at history, at the ways in which black women's bodies have been treated and are continually treated, it is easy for me to look on this past and believe she was raped—that her children and their children and ultimately my own reason for existence, is because of this. It is easier to simplify their history, to make black and white a situation I don't understand, but there is a fact that keeps me questioning, one I come back to time and time again. At least two of the children, born during Reconstruction, took his surname.

This fact leads me to believe that there is perhaps a different story than the one I'd originally believed.

"Even still," my godmother says on the phone. I have called her again, as I periodically do when I need to ask another question about our past, or when in my scattered research stumble across another detail, another piece. She is a history professor and in my family is the only one I know left who can offer any clues or advice. "Even still, she was a woman and she was black. How much power could she have had, really?"

We are the only two black people in this bar. Typically, this is something I try not to pay attention to. In college I was the only black female in all of my classes and during graduate school I was the only black person until the last class before I graduated. In my doctorate program, I am one of five other black students—two I rarely ever see on campus, me, and two new students, one of which is the man I am now meeting. With him though I am made aware. Experience has taught me that when you are the anomaly in your life's surroundings you teach yourself to ignore it. With him though, I begin questioning the side glances of the others around us as we settle into our seats. The smirk of the bartender after I try to get his attention—or was it just my imagination? There is a heightened awareness to every interaction, and yet still I fear misjudging the situation. When the bartender fails to bring back my tequila, when after taking my card he goes to make several other drinks from the people sitting near me, I remind myself that my annoyance is an overreaction, and even if it was justified, I should hold my tongue. Every action, every moment is an opportunity to prove that I am something more than the possible assumptions and beliefs of my race, and so I am patient and I smile and eventually my drink does come.

The prevalent "darky" icon, popular in 19th-century post-Civil War comic strips, ads, cartoons, books, and toys, was depicted with skin the color of ink, had bright white teeth, wide open eyes, and deep red lips. The darky was nostalgic for the old South, before war had destroyed his plantation home.

Blackface minstrelsy used the image of the "happy-go-lucky darky" in their caricatured portrayals of African Americans. Blackface helped propagate other stereotypes that have been long-lasting in our culture— the buck, the Uncle Tom, the Zip Coon, the pickaninny, and for women, the tragic mulatta, the mammy, and the wench/jezebel.

In blackface minstrelsy, the jezebel was promiscuous and immoral. She was a temptress, a counter depiction to the pure, modest, and self-controlled white woman. "Black women are jezebels," was the excuse slave owners gave when they raped them.

The jezebel archetype far precedes its 19th-century application to black women. In the Bible, Jezebel was the wife of King Ahab of Israel. She was a Phoenician who worshipped gods other than Yahweh. She used her influence on her husband to spread idol worship of her gods Baal and Asherah in Israel. Jezebel was murdered by the general Jehu, who after overtaking their land and the anointed king ordered her eunuchs to throw her out the palace window. Because she was an idolater and a temptress, she was killed, her body consumed by dogs.

Of course, there is another way of looking at her story. Jezebel was a foreigner in a new land, a woman ethnically different, an Other. While standing at her watchtower in Jezreel, she witnessed the murder of her son Joram from Jehu's planned coup against Ahab's dynasty. She knew that for Jehu to succeed, he would have to murder every member of Ahab's family, and as Jehu made his way to Jezreel, Jezebel dressed herself in the makeup and head-dress of her gods. Her makeup and adornments were not last-ditch efforts of seduction but an attempt to meet her death with dignity, to die being seen as what she rightfully was—a queen.

The man I have come here to meet is gregarious and warm. At one point during the evening he offers to stand, giving up his seat so another couple can sit together, but when one of them looks and sees me she declines. "You were here already," she says, despite his protests.

"I'm pretty docile in my personality," he tells me afterward as a sort of explanation. "You know, black man in a white college town and all. I guess you have to be."

"I understand," I say.

He asks me what it's like living in this town, and I struggle to find an answer. I don't know him well enough to tell him the truth. I don't explain about the program, about the casual racism present despite my false assumption our peers should behave better. I also don't mention the overt racism prevalent not just in the town but in the surrounding areas.

"Where'd you live before here?" I ask instead, changing the subject.

"California," he says.

"You should have stayed in California."

"Racism exists there too."

"Yeah, I know, but better weather."

"True," he says, nodding. "You know what? It doesn't seem that bad here. I mean, I could be wrong, but it seems mostly okay?"

Because I can't take it anymore, I tell him about the cotton balls. Two students who were arrested for putting cotton balls in front of the Black Culture Center on campus. I tell him about the slurs spray-painted to mock Black History Month. I tell him about the swastika drawn on the wall in one of the dorms. There is a tension on the campus, I say, and it has existed for quite a while, even before I came here, and it is building.

It has not happened yet, but in a few weeks that tension will reach a breaking point with protests that will make national news, heightening the ways in which I perceive myself to be seen.

"It's not that bad though, or maybe I've just gotten used to it all," I finally answer, and he laughs, seeing immediately through my lie.

For black women, if you're not the Jezebel then you are the mammy, desexualized but still an object. Always, you are the object, maybe not of sexual desire, but still a reduction of who you are.

Never mind that the idea of the mammy—dark-skinned, overweight, and middle-aged—is a construction having no real basis in history. Female house slaves during slavery were light-skinned, of mixed race, and thin. They weren't old considering that fewer than ten percent of black women lived beyond fifty years of age. The caricature that's been so culturally ingrained—from the image of Aunt Jemima popular on pancake mixes for decades, to Hattie McDaniel's portrayal in *Gone With the Wind*—were, and have always been, fictions created to soothe.

We are Jezebels or we are mammies, or we are Sapphires or tragic mulattas. We are the gold-digger, the angry black woman, or the welfare queen. Object or abject, we are always one or the other, but always considered an Other.

"So have you dated anyone here?"

"No," I say, already feeling defensive.

"No one?"

"No."

He pushes for an answer as to why, an answer I'm unwilling to give. It's too early in the evening for such a conversation. A few weeks earlier I was at a bar and a man, in his mid-forties, came up to order a drink. He smiled and said hello in my direction and out of politeness I nodded back. This provoked him to conversation and then to offer to buy me another unasked-for drink.

"You know," he said, leaning closer, "I've always liked the coloreds. I've always wanted to date one."

These men aren't unusual. They aren't specific to Missouri where I am now, but have been in Massachusetts and North Carolina and Kentucky, all the places I've lived. They are sometimes older, men who want to reenact some racial fantasy of their dreams, but sometimes they are younger, curious about what it's like.

It is tiring, I want to say, all the ways in which you're seen.

"I guess there aren't many black people here to date," he says.

"No, there aren't."

Perhaps this is why I have dolled myself up for this. Because for the first time in a long while I'd be on a date where I knew I wouldn't be made to feel like an object. For an evening I would be with someone who understands our history, who understands what it's like to navigate this world. Perhaps this is why I had stayed so long in front of the bathroom mirror, and why I had taken out that tube of lipstick, putting it on carefully, wanting for the first time in a long while for my intention to be known.

But in the end I had smeared my lips clean. Too afraid in the end, even to someone who might understand, of how it might appear.

Saturday mornings I get in my car and drive. There's an antique store just on the outskirts of the Missouri town in which I live, and to kill some of the hours of my day I decide to go.

There in the middle of the store is a doll. Black onyx skin. Wide red lips. Knotted black hair. A pickaninny doll. I'm so taken aback that I stop and stare at it. The doll is predominantly displayed on top of a chest of drawers for sale.

The male clerk at the front of the store catches me staring. "You thinking about buying it?" he asks.

"I don't know."

"It looks pretty taken care of. Good condition."

This exchange is too much. He is unaware of the symbolism of the doll, of what it signifies, or maybe he is perhaps pretending in an attempt to make a sale.

"I think I'm going to pass," I tell him.

"You sure? You seem like you want it."

"Yeah, I'm sure," I say, and then head for the door.

The next day I go back and thankfully someone else is working. I pay for the doll quickly, saying as little as possible to the clerk as she places it in a plastic bag.

I bought the doll for the sole purpose of trashing it. I wanted to feel some sort of vindication as I took it apart, disassembled its limbs, cut to shreds the fabric of its clothes, but when I got it home I couldn't do it. How often our history has been erased, sanitized, perverted and disguised. The ugliness forgotten and what's left is its echo reverberating in all the ways we are forced to understand ourselves.

I don't get rid of the doll. Instead, I put it in a box in my closet where it sits now.

I'm not sure I'll ever have children, but if I do one day when they're older I'll take the doll out and say, "Look. This is how they used to see you. This was what they thought of us. Do you understand? So you must always be careful, always be aware of how the world sees you, will continue to see you. It's not right, but like anything, it is what it is."

Leanna Brown's death certificate says she died of "tragic burns to the neck and shoulders." This detail has kept me awake at night—the grotesque images it conjures because of the description's simplicity. I've spent far too long considering the different possibilities in an attempt to understand, but there is no understanding such a horror, no matter the answer.

"You might never know, and you're going to have to be okay with that," my godmother says when I call her to tell her about this new piece of information.

I'm not ready for such a resolution, not of her death nor of the mysteries surrounding her life. I'm not ready for her to be forgotten like so many have been and are continuing to be.

I can't imagine what it must have been like to have spent a month living in a body that didn't feel like her own, but how much of her body was ever her own? Considering the time, and the place, her life, how much agency could she have ever had?

This, I wonder.

Leanna lived for a month suffering from her burns before dying. She is buried in Rose Hill off of Highway 58. She has no tombstone.

My phone vibrates in my pocket. I ignore it the first time and the second, but the third time I know it'll continue unless I answer.

"I'm sorry," I say, quickly taking my phone out to check the messages.

"You're popular."

"Not really."

As I thought, it's my best friend messaging me about tonight. He is wanting to know how it's going, if it will continue. If I don't respond he'll assume this has led to sex, and later, tomorrow morning, he'll message asking me to talk about it.

"You're such a prude," he will say when I don't answer, and when I chastise him for it he'll stop, but hanging in the air of our conversations will be this absence of the things I won't say and the misunderstanding as to why.

There is a saying that a woman decides within the first few minutes of meeting a man if she wants to sleep with him, and even though I have decided there is a difference between desire and action, between what one wants and what one is willing to do, I know that no matter how the night swings I will go home alone.

As I sit across from this man though I wonder if maybe it is really the expectation of desire, that because we are here and we are the same race, these factors alone should be enough to warrant it, and just as quickly as I have made my decision I am now beginning to question the motivation behind my want.

When I look at my skin and remember the history, it goes down easier to believe that maybe Leanna's relationship with this man was consensual because otherwise how do you make peace with such a past? How does one move on when the legacy is evident from a simple glance in the mirror?

I'm afraid that if the relationship was not consensual that her life becomes reduced to an archetype, but I must remember she was more than just an archetype. She was a woman who lived her life the best she could. She was a woman who managed to provide her children with the name of their father, so they would always know some semblance of their history. She was a woman who died a tragic death but not before fighting for her life all the way until the end.

Consider the woman known as Saartjie Baartman, or "little Sara" in Dutch. Saartjie Baartman's birth name is unknown. The world knows her as Saartjie, or "little Sara," the diminutive name establishing her status and her difference. Born on the southernmost tip of South Africa, known in the 18th and early 19th centuries as the Cape of Good Hope. She belonged to the heterogeneous indigenous group, the Khoikhoi. Dubbed the Hottentot Venus, her body was put on exhibition in London, displayed as a sexual curiosity, a freak of nature due to her size.

At No. 225 Piccadilly, members of the public could pay two shillings to view the "Hottentot Venus." Up on a stage Baartman was made to walk, stand, or sit as she was led around by her keeper. She wore a skin-tight "dress resembling her complexion" to give the appearance of being undressed.

Four years after arriving in London, she was indentured to the animal trainer S. Réaux. S. Réaux displayed Baartman in Paris, drawing the attention of Parisian scientists, most specifically that of Georges Cuvier, who requested S. Réaux give a private showing. For three days Cuvier, along with an assortment of anatomists, zoologists, and physiologists, examined Baartman's anatomy.

After she died, an artist was commissioned to make a plaster molding of her body, considered to be of "special scientific interest". Baartman was dissected at the *Muséum d'Histoire Naturelle* in front of an audience of scientists. Her skeleton was removed. Her brain and genitals extracted and pickled in jars. Her organs were submitted to the French Academy of Sciences. She was put on display at the *Muséum d'Histoire Naturelle* up until 1937 when Paris's *Musée de l'Homme* was founded. Her remains and the plaster molding were displayed there up until the late 1970s.

Gold inscriptions of the French poet, Paul Valery, adorn the upper facade of the *Musée de l'Homme*. "Rare or beautiful things are wisely gathered here," the English translation of one of the inscriptions begins, "teach the eye to see all things in the world as if never seen before."

"I'm going to go back there," I tell my godmother one night. "I'm going to go back and see if I can find the records, but also to see the land—the plantation Leanna lived on. I need to see it."

"I don't know why I've never tried. I've thought about doing it, not just trying to figure that out but really sitting down and outlining the whole line but—"

"But what?"

"Life, I think," she says. "Plus there's just too much trauma in that story I couldn't bring myself to deal with it. Who knows anyway, maybe this task was always meant for you."

If I'm honest with myself, this is not a task I want. I am not a historian. I know very little about archival research, and the idea of driving back to that area worries me, especially going alone. I also do not want to dwell in this past. It is too much to think about the injustices of my ancestors, but I find that despite my protests certain questions continue to infiltrate my life. I find myself circling back, and I know that the only way to get some sense of peace is to go.

"If you do end up going there you should also look into what your Uncle Pete said happened with the land. I've always wondered if what he said was true even though now I'm starting to believe that he was right."

My godmother has brought this up a few times before. Her father, my great-uncle, had always argued that some of their land was stolen. After the death of his father, a couple of men came to the house asking his mother to see the deed. At the time she was a woman living alone with eight children in an area heavily dominated by the Klan, and out of fear she relented and gave them the deed. The men took it and when it was given back it was altered, changed to reflect less than half their number of acres.

I tell her about Ta-Nehisi Coates and his essay "The Case for Reparations." "*Yes*, I want reparations," she says, light-heartedly, although deep down

I know she's serious. "Yes, reparations for everything. All we lost. Someone should give him my number because I even know how it could be done."

I do not need to tell you of all the ways in which black women's bodies have been violated. From the auction block as women were stripped down, their bodies laid bare for the world to see and consume. The skin oiled so that it gleamed underneath the sun. The body was poked and prodded under the guise of an examination. Slave owners would knead women's stomachs in an attempt to determine how many children they'd have. Some were subjected to experimental gynecological exams. They were sold and bought for breeding purposes, and those who couldn't were beaten. The body classified and categorized.

Or the decades of rape. We remember Betty Jean Owens, Recy Taylor, and we say never again.

I do not need to explain about the more than 64,000 missing black women and children that have disappeared and the lack of investigations and the lack of outrage.

Or the decades of state-sponsored sterilizations of black and other women of color. A woman named Elaine Riddick was raped when she was thirteen. She was sterilized without her consent after the child was born. In the state eugenics board's records she is described as "promiscuous," using that as the basis for why she should be sterilized.

Perhaps you too are tired of seeing the images, of listening to these stories, and don't need to hear me tell you about Daniel Holtzclaw, about his serial raping of at least thirteen black women. He preyed on them because they were poor and because they were black, because he had power and they had none, and because he knew, and what he convinced them to also believe, was that the world would not care.

I do not need to explain about the ways in which our bodies have been taken, have been handled without our consent, have been objectified, appropriated, or stolen. I do not need to tell you—but I will.

"So where are you from?" the man I'm with asks, trying again to change the subject. "What about your family? Where are they?"

"My mother grew up in a small unincorporated community near the Virginia border."

"Oh really? Where?"

To make things easier, I tell him one of the nearby towns. "Yanceyville," I say, then broadening my answer to tell him the county. "It's in Caswell County, up near the Virginia border."

Even those I've met from North Carolina often don't know of where I mean, and so I say all this expecting him to nod and then move on as so many others in the past have done, but instead he holds my gaze. "I know Yanceyville," he says. "I know it well. My father preached there when I was a child."

"So did my grandfather," I say. "When was this?"

"During the 70s."

"So around the same time. Do you think they knew each other? I mean, they would have had to, right? They must have. We're not talking about a big city here. They were both preachers to the same community."

"Yes. They probably did."

The coincidence of this, of two strangers coming together in such a way, will keep me wondering, and also the meaning, if there is one, behind the odds of such a thing happening.

"I'll ask him when I can."

'Your father's still alive?"

"Yes."

I know now this will bond us in a way nothing else ever would. We are two black people in academia, that alone would have been enough, but now there is the possibility of the connection between our ancestors. He says we are kindred, and the antiquatedness of the word makes me want to laugh, but I know he's right.

The bar is crowded now, forcing us to sit even closer together, the act forming an intimacy among strangers.

He waves for the bartender and asks for Hennessey but the bartender shrugs and says they don't have it. This doesn't surprise me. We are in a college town, after all, a world of watered-down whiskey and cokes and vodka tonics. He pauses, then tells the bartender he'll have to think a moment longer before deciding what else to order.

"I know it's a stereotype to drink it," he tells me later, "but whatever. I like the taste. I am who I am."

He gives a self-conscious laugh after this that lets me know despite what he says he too deep down is battling the same insecurities.

We never escape it, I think, this fear we are conceding to our depictions, to the world's assumptions and misconceptions. Our past is always there, coming to define and redefine who we are to each other.

"You want to go to another bar?"

"No, we can stay here awhile longer," he says, and watches as I slowly sip my tequila.

We're both quiet now, and in the silence he shifts his weight on the barstool. His hand touches my knee in the process, an accidental transgression, and even though it should not be on my mind I can't help but think of the image of the two of us to an onlooker. I wish I could say that I am not suddenly ashamed, that I do not blush or turn to look and see if we are noticed. As I glance around the room, I try to remind myself that we are just a couple in a bar having a drink, and that if one were to turn and look they would only see two people, each of them cautious and fumbling, who are continuously learning how to be.

# After Water Comes the Fire

A friend of mine can taste the differences in bottled water. We're friends of circumstance, the two of us having become close after I'd moved to Missouri for graduate school. I'd gone over her apartment to study with her when I commented on the containers upon containers of empty gallon jugs she kept in her kitchen. That's when she told me about the water. She said she always bought her water because there was only a specific brand she was able to drink. It must go through reverse osmosis, she said. It must not have fluoride. It must be purified.

"You're full of it. Water is water," I told her, and then I called her elitist. I was irritated even though I knew deep down my irritation stemmed not from the water but in how it marked the differences between us. She's white and Republican, and I am not. She's the kind of religious I used to be, the church on Sunday mornings and Bible study during the week kind of religious I've now forgone. Whereas I grew up the product of divorced parents who scraped and pinched to afford my childhood and adolescence, her family was upper middle class.

That evening I decided to call my friend's bluff. As an experiment I went out and bought all the popular brands of bottled water to test and then I brought them back to her apartment. I poured two fingers full of each into clear glasses and placed them all in front of her. Dasani. Poland Springs. Aquafina. Fiji. Voss. "Okay, tell me which is which," I said when I was finished.

To my surprise she got them all correct. "Well, I'll be damned," I said.

"Told you."

I responded by saying we were going again. "Just to make sure," I said, collecting the glasses off of her kitchen table.

In the Book of Matthew, John the Baptist went to the people of Judea to preach repentance. Many in the surrounding regions came to see him and to be baptized. When the Pharisees and the Sadducees appeared, John stopped his baptism. He believed that these two groups were hypocrites, wanting merely to appear repentant while not truly believing. John explained that even though he would baptize them with the water, someone else was coming, another mightier than him who would baptize with the Holy Spirit and with fire. The fire referred to the coming judgment of those who have not repented.

This lesson should be enough to convince me, but I've still not been baptized. My mother believed it should be a choice and I never made the choice. As a child, I watched as my friends completed the necessary ritual. Every Sunday another one would go up to the pulpit, and I watched the ceremony from my pew. I watched as the pastor held them as they leaned back. I watched as he let them fall into the water, and when he brought them back up, I listened as the congregation rejoiced.

My mother had worked as a church secretary. She'd quit a few weeks earlier, came home and told me she was done. Earlier that afternoon the pastor had gone out to lunch with another woman, and when his wife called my mother had told the truth as to where he'd been. Later, when the pastor found out, my mother was reprimanded for it, and was told to lie to her in the future if need be, and so she quit.

As I'd looked up at the pulpit I knew I couldn't do what everyone else expected. To me it seemed like a ritual, nothing more, and they'd done it for the sake of the rite of passage. For me it was not enough of a reason. I waited until I thought I'd be ready and then discovered I never was.

The year my parents divorced my mother took me to the local community center for swimming lessons. For an hour every weekday an instructor taught a group of others and me how to swim. We learned how to bob, how to float from the front and back, and how to flutter kick. Towards the end the instructor taught us the front crawl and the backstroke.

I would only take lessons there that one time, enough to swim but not to be any good. As part of the divorce I would spend every summer thereafter with my father. He would assume I'd learned enough enrolled me instead in a day camp for the children of military families. Every afternoon a school bus carted us off to a nearby pool where for an hour we'd swim. There was a swimming test and those who passed were allowed to cross the white line and swim in the deep end. I watched from the shallow side as other kids took turns doing elaborate flips from the diving board, falling into the dark water below.

One summer I finally told myself I would take the test. I pushed myself as far as I could go, telling myself I would at least complete the test so I could say I tried, but really I wanted to pass. I wanted to join the others, to feel included for once in my life. I wanted to dive from that diving board. Halfway through the test my body got tired and I switched my body position. I turned on my back, closed my eyes, and floated, briefly remembering my lessons from the past year. I stared up at the sun before closing my eyes. I back-paddled but not with the same effort.

I heard the whistle of the lifeguard. When I opened my eyes I saw him standing at the side of the pool. He told me I had to stop what I was doing, that it was either swim or give up. I only had a few minutes left so I needed to make a decision.

"I'm done," I yelled, quitting. I swam to the pool's edge. I knew I would never try again, not this summer or anytime after. I got out, dried off, and when he told me I wouldn't get the band I only shook my head.

When I was a kid I almost drowned. My mother had decided to take the daughter of a friend along with me to a water park. I had not wanted to go. Despite the fact that her family attended the same church I didn't know the girl who'd be joining us very well. My mother was always trying to get us together in the hope that we'd be friends and this trip was another one of those attempts.

"Why do we have to be friends?" I'd asked her beforehand. "I don't think she likes me anyway."

"She likes you. Why would you say that? Of course she does."

At the water park, we decided to go into the wave pool, with both of us carrying opposite ends of a double tube to take to the water. My mother watched from the sidelines. "Just for a little bit," she'd said absentmindedly, already looking for shade to shield her sensitive skin from the sun.

I did not want to be here but my mother had insisted. I did not want to go in the water, not really. I wanted to sit under the sun, but I knew I couldn't opt out of participating. "Be nice," my mother had told me earlier, her warning, and that meant acquiescing to what she wanted. Not wanting her to be angry I nodded and went along as I climbed onto the tube and let myself be pulled by the water.

Our tube slowly moved toward the deeper end. Soon we passed the eight-foot mark, then the ninth, and the tenth. I was still not a good swimmer, despite the lessons and the practice, and the farther we got the more crowded it became, the waves knocking the tubes against each other.

"We should go back!" I yelled.

"Why?"

I knew it was coming before it happened. I saw the manipulated wave, knew in the few seconds before it hit us it would turn our tube over, that soon I would be deep in the water struggling to breathe, struggling to find the surface, the light.

What I've remembered was after—the lifeguard standing above me after having pulled me out, his face red from a mix of exertion and fear, my mother standing behind him in the background, worry wrinkling her face before the expression quickly dissolved.

"What happened?" I asked my mother, coughing, my chest hurting.

"What happened is that it's time to go home."

After the pool, my father would get off of work and come pick me up. Together we'd go to the grocery store to get dinner. Even then my father nickeled and dimed. It's a character trait I've learned to accept over the years, but when I was a child I was impatient in his need to price compare, and I was not understanding of his habit of always buying the cheapest product.

While waiting in the checkout line my father said he was thirsty. "Well, there's water," I told him, pointing to the cases by the register filled with racks of bottled water. I went and picked out the cheapest bottle and held it up for him to take.

My father looked at me and laughed. "You've got to be kidding," he said. "How much money do you think I have to waste?" He told me to wait where I stood, and I watched as he walked a couple of feet to a nearby water fountain.

I was too young then to recognize how he saw this choice as a privilege. My father, who grew up in the segregated south, who grew up using black designated facilities, of learning to navigate the black only and white only spaces of everything, and then who witnessed the violence from desegregation. It did not occur to me the meaning behind his choice.

"Free always tastes better," he said, smiling as he wiped his mouth dry.

It's been over a decade since I've swum. Sometimes I've thought that maybe I should try again considering how long public pools across the country were segregated. It's easy to understand the ways in which this has shaped future generations' relationships to water. The amount of African American children who can't swim is almost double the rate of white children, and African American children drown at nearly three times the overall rate. The legacy of segregation still continues, and maybe this was why my mother tried so hard to make sure I'd learn.

In a photo album once belonging to my mother is a picture of a man known in my family to have passed for white. With his dark hair slicked back, he's posed sitting on the edge of a swimming pool.

This man wanted to become an actor, or so our folklore goes, and he made a decision and left his family behind. I've heard the stories of when he'd come back to visit, how he'd take multiple cabs, for example, before finally deciding on being brought to the black section where his mother lived. The photo I have was given to the family during one of these visits. It was passed down to my mother and after she died, passed on to me.

I don't know his name, not what it once was or what it became. I do not know if he was successful in his dream or if in life he pursued something else. All I have, all I know, is this image of him and all of what it signifies.

"Do you know who this is?" I asked my godmother once. She's the only link in my family who might provide answers to such questions. She said she remembered the picture I was talking about, said that she too might have a copy somewhere in her house if she were to look, but she'd also forgotten the man's name.

"I'm not even sure I'd know who to ask to try and find out about it," she said.

"It's okay," I told her. "I just find it interesting that he'd send a photo of him at the pool."

"Well, remember black people often couldn't go to pools back then. They were segregated, and so it would have been a big deal for the rest of the family to see that, to see a photo of him at a pool. It would have meant he was somebody."

I've heard it said that the next world war would be brought on by water. Across the world huge areas are drying up, and the combination of drought and water shortages will heighten existing conflicts between countries. Water will be, as Goldman Sachs described it, "the petroleum of the next century."

During the last year of my Master's there was a water ban in Boston. A water pipe broke and began flooding the Charles River. The Governor declared a state of emergency and ordered that all the drinking water must be boiled.

Panic spread across the city. Restaurants closed, posting signs across the front of their doors that they weren't accepting patrons for the rest of the evening. Drugstores, running out of bottled water to sell, filled the front of their coolers with Coke products, hoping to further their profits. Before I took the subway home I stopped in the downtown Shaw's, the grocery store situated in Copley Mall known for being one of the city's wealthier shopping districts. While in the store I debated what to buy, how much I could even afford to spend on water. I watched as Back Bay shoppers filled their shopping carts with bottled water. They were frantic, desperate as they cleaned the store out.

A woman next to me in the aisle was filling her cart with gallon jugs. She emptied the counter and then caught the expression on my face from staring. "I need it to bathe," she said as explanation.

"I thought the concern was with drinking it, and even then we can still boil the water though, right? It's okay if we boil it I thought?"

"I just want to be safe," the woman answered as she pulled her cart away. "I don't want to take any chances."

The summer after I left Boston and moved to Missouri it was hot, every day reaching the triple digits. Even a few minutes outside in the heat felt unbearable, and because of this I tried to wait until late in the evening to do my errands, until the sun had already set, giving an illusion in a drop in temperature, but always the thick headiness of the air remained.

"Did you see them?" my neighbor asked me one such night. She was watering the plants on her deck when she caught me. She was older, a retiree like most of the residents in my complex, and she spent most of her day sitting on her desk, watching as the rest of us came and went.

"Who?" I asked.

"Those kids."

"I didn't notice," I said, although I had. The fence bordering our pool wasn't locked. The pool was small, more of a wading pool than anything else, and in the few weeks I'd been living here I'd rarely seen anyone else use it which was why when I'd heard the noise I'd gone to my window to see, had looked out and saw the group of black kids in the water.

"They've got nothing else better to do so they sneak over here late at night and use our pool."

I was struck then on her use of our—*our* pool, and I wondered how much of it was intentional.

"I had to kick them out," she said. "They just had no respect at all."

"Why does it matter if no one uses it?"

"That's not the point."

The point was the principle of the matter. They were not part of the complex and shouldn't be able to use the facilities. It was an argument I understood but didn't agree with, because standing there listening to her I was sweating through my clothes. With each second I felt as if heat stroke was coming, and I looked out at the empty pool and it seemed like wasted effort to be up in arms.

"Next time I'm calling the cops," my neighbor said. I left her to finish watering her plants, knowing full well that she would.

I never saw the neighborhood kids in the pool again. The summer heat acquiesced to fall and throughout all that time the pool stayed mostly empty except for the occasional sunbather.

Despite the months passing, I couldn't get used to Missouri or the town and I spent most of my time in my apartment. I learned to get used to the quiet and each week I settled more into the realization of my loneliness. By winter I preferred it, and so it came as a surprise when I heard a knocking at my door. It was freezing out and I opened the door to find two men who'd come to proselytize. They wanted to give me a Bible lesson, explained how it would only take a few minutes, and I wasn't sure why but I let them. Maybe it was because of their sheepish expressions, their defenses being down from having so many previous doors slammed in their face. They seemed happy and surprised I'd taken the time. I didn't let them in and we all stood in my doorway in the cold while they asked me to read out loud passages from their Bible.

Five minutes went by. Ten. Soon I couldn't feel my toes in my slippers. We were all shivering. They were having a hard time turning the thin pages of the Bible. Their teeth chattered as they asked me to read each marked verse.

"It's so cold. Do you guys want to just come back and do this another time?" I finally interrupted, knowing once I closed the door I was never opening it again. They seemed to sense this too, that there would never be another time, and so they said they'd continue.

"Okay, well, do you think we can wrap this up maybe?"

They got to their point and asked me if I'd been baptized and I told them the truth. They asked, well do you know what will happen to your soul? They asked, don't you want to accept Jesus in your heart? Don't you want eternal salvation? They said they could baptize me. They even had a baptism bus.

"What does that mean, a baptism bus?"

They wanted to bring it and show me, they said. It wouldn't take long. They could bring it right now so I could be baptized.

"I—" I stalled, trying to figure out a way out, but they were unwilling to let this go. I thought back to my mother's desire and how I would wait until I was ready.

I told them okay even though once they left I would already be gone, already getting in my car and driving away so as not to be there when they came back. Still, for a moment I believed maybe it was time, that maybe I was ready, and so I told them to bring the bus and they both nodded, grinning from ear to ear.

During the 1840's in Petersburg, Virginia, a physician by the name of Walter F. Jones once used slaves to test a remedy for typhoid pneumonia. The patient was put on the floor, face down, while five gallons of boiling water were thrown immediately on the spine. Every couple of hours this process was repeated. According to Jones, this process helped patients recover by "re-establishing the capillary circulation."

Decades later in the mine camps belonging to Joel Hurt, the wealthy Atlanta real estate developer and investor, slaves were tortured with what was known as the "water cure," a punishment in which water was poured into the nostrils and lungs of prisoners. It was preferred to whipping because it allowed miners to "go to work right away" after being punished.

In the narrative of his life as a slave, Charles Ball described a time when his master explained to him how he'd found a mode of punishment "much more mild" than whipping. He told Ball to come to the house and there he showed him the water pump. Ball watched as another slave was stripped naked, was tied to a post so that her head was underneath the stream of water that began to pour, and she was given the "punishment of the pump."

During the Civil Rights Movement, Birmingham's Commissioner of Public Safety Eugene "Bull" Connor directed the police department to use high-pressure water hoses on nonviolent protestors. Police aimed the water hoses on children who'd formed their bodies into balls so the pressure wouldn't sting, but the water was forceful enough to wash them down the street where they were met with dogs or batons.

It's difficult to not be reminded of all the ways water has harmed. The EPA estimates that 90,000 public schools and half a million child-care facilities aren't regulated under the Safe Drinking Act. When I lived in Boston, three-quarters of the public schools didn't even have access to traditional water fountains. When I worked at an at-risk after-school program housed at one of these public schools, kids got their water from five-gallon coolers, and often they ran out. In Flint and Newark and Maine and California and in hundreds of other schools across our country children are being exposed to tainted water. Children have died, and most likely will continue to die, because of lack of access to what I believe should be a right.

Like Hughes, I could speak to you not just of rivers but also of all the vessels of water. There were the oceans that brought us here. We were chained two by two on slave ships. When the tight quarters on the Zong made us ill, when disease spread through the ship like wildfire, like spoiled cargo we were thrown overboard. Some of us sacrificed ourselves to the ocean's depths, choosing our own deaths rather than submit to such a massacre. On the Moravia we rose up, refusing our awaiting fate of forced labor, and when the ship landed on the Georgia shore, we walked together back into the water that had brought us. The water became our salvation, taking us to our promised land, giving us back our power in this new world where we'd have none.

The rivers we were once sold down, down the Mississippi or the Ohio, our River Jordan, as we were transported to the cotton plantations where we'd work until our deaths. On river boats we served as deck hands, cabin boys, and stevedores. We escaped on these rivers in the ferries we operated. We waded in the waters as we hid from our captors. We took ships like the Pearl and sailed south down the Potomac, then north on the Delaware in our hope for freedom.

I could speak to you on all the ways in which water has flowed through our history. Oceans have washed away our blood. Rivers have cleansed away our sins. Water once nourished our spirits and guided us to salvation. Water has harmed but also saved, and it will continue to make us anew.

Easter Sunday and my father called to check in. "I was in the car coming from church and I was thinking about this story your godmother told me once about when the two of them were children. You know their farms were close by, and one day she came to her all excited. She went and pulled her from the field and asked her if she was saved. Your godmother said yes but your mother responded by saying that wasn't enough. 'You gotta believe,' she'd told her."

This was him asking, I knew. He wanted me to be saved so I could avoid the fate awaiting me for not repenting, but I thought of all the ways those who were once saved have used the Bible for countless atrocities and injustices. I knew my father's response to this would be to say that hypocrites are nonbelievers, that other's actions shouldn't dictate one's belief or one's choice, and as much as I understood this I couldn't help but wonder what I would believe after I were to go down to that water, and I knew that merely completing the ritual would never be enough.

I didn't respond to my father, instead listened as his laughter from the story died down. "Even then she was so forceful," he said after a brief moment of silence, "but then she always sort of was about her convictions."

"Did you know it's been ten years? Since mom?"

"Ten years? It feels like less than that. Four or five maybe."

My father and I have never been close but since my mother's death we have become closer. We were two people who each live alone, who would perhaps continue to live the rest of our lives alone. Our acceptance of this, that in the end we were all the other one had, was what brought us together.

"Could mom swim?" I suddenly asked, changing the subject.

"No, I don't think so," he said, his voice picking up again. "Growing up there wouldn't have been anyplace for her to have learned how. I taught myself in the pond with all those snakes and goodness knows what else— the things you do as a kid you look back and realize how dumb they were."

"At least you learned."

"Yeah," he said. "It's good you learned too."

A few blocks from my apartment there's a community center with an indoor pool. It would take me two years before I decided to use it, two years of living in this town for me to embolden myself with the task of buying a bathing suit and convincing myself of the endeavor, and one evening when most of the neighborhood kids were already home eating dinner and the nine-to-fivers were downtown drinking, I got in my car and went.

Inside, I passed the basketball courts with kids shooting hoops and I snuck inside the nearby changing room. I was uncomfortable in my swimsuit the moment I put it on. The fabric itched and I was self-conscious over so much of myself being exposed. My body was not the same as it once was and my insecurity remained. I tried to put it aside as I glanced at my dimpled thighs or at the roundness of my stomach. I tried not to think of my hair, now tied in a bun at the nape of my neck, as I put the cap over my head.

I left the changing room and went to find the pool. I was lucky that there were only a few people there, each of them focused on swimming in their own lanes. I slipped into the water. I felt the shock of its coldness the moment the water hit my skin and I suppressed a yelp. As I floated near the pool's edge I knew I wouldn't be any good and for a moment I wondered what was the point, but then I remembered the way I'd floated in the water long ago. I remembered the cough-choke-burn in my chest from that afternoon at the park. I remembered the image of my relative smiling beside the pool. I remembered the decades of history where something as small as this was once denied.

My goal was to do a mile. Thirty laps. I breathed in quickly before pushing my body through the water. One stroke and then another, I told myself. It was a matter of moving forward, of not looking back, it was a matter of breathing, and so I swam. I made one lap and then turned and made another. It wasn't long before I was tired but I would finish. One stroke and another and another, I thought. My arms continuing to pull my body forward, struggling, and each time as my head turned up to the surface, to the air and the light, I remembered to take a breath.

# And Lest You Forget[1]

Introduction to Columbia: The Missouri city of Columbia,[2] located in Boone County,[3] is home to the University of Missouri[4] as well as Columbia College and Stephens College. The city lies in the heart of the state, almost equidistant from Kansas City (127 miles to the west) and St. Louis (124 miles to the east).

- Historic Old Southwest Neighborhood.[5] The magazine of the Mizzou Alumni Association notes that this an eclectic area west

---

1. Or, originally, "Points of Interest."

2. Little Dixie, they used to call this area, this region consisting of between six to seventeen counties in the middle part of Missouri. Named Little Dixie because here the attitudes and beliefs aligned with those of the antebellum South. Here in this region slaves made up as much as 50% of the population, the largest numbers belonging to plantations close to the Missouri River.

3. While the exact boundaries have been up for debate, there are six counties considered to be the "heart" of Little Dixie—Audrain, Callaway, Howard, Monroe, Randolph, and Boone. During the "nadir" of race relations, the period of history between the end of Reconstruction through to the early 20th century, there were thirteen lynchings of black men in these counties. At least two of them happened not just in Boone County but in Columbia.

4. You left Boston, where you'd lived for the past ten years, and moved to Columbia for a graduate program. You are hoping for a fresh start.

5. The "professorial ghetto" a professor will jokingly explain early on in your time here.

of the University of Missouri campus that "shelters many MU Professors,[6] local professionals and some old-money Columbia families."[7]

---

6. You'll take a class with this professor. Only one. A few weeks before it begins, a friend of yours in the program will come to you and explain how she's got a funny story to tell. She was in his office and they were looking at the photos of the people in the class.

"What photos?"

"The ID ones. They're the ones on the roster."

She says that he showed her the list. They were going down it and when he got to your photo he stopped and said, "Look at her face. Look at that one. She's going to be trouble. Just you watch."

"What the hell? Why would he say that?"

"Oh come on. It was just a joke. It's because of your photo, your face."

"What about my photo? What about my face makes me look like I'm trouble?"

She will laugh off your concern, change the subject, but apparently there is something wrong with your face. Your expression too harsh. Perhaps it's because you don't smile as often as you should, or because you don't uptalk at the end of your sentences and so every word uttered is implied as being angry. It's because you're too quiet, that you take too long to think, to articulate, and in the span of time between what you want to say and what you actually do say others' perceptions of you changes. Your pause for clarity turns into meaning a pause of judgment.

So you are always revising—how you should act, what you should say, how you should be. You continue being silent. You accommodate. You make the smallest version of yourself you could possibly make but still it's never enough because your face is still your face and no matter how you're seen that will never change.

7. A gathering for new students is being held at another professor's house. You're still unfamiliar with the area and even with GPS you're not sure which unmarked house it's supposed to be. You think, well if you could just get out and—and what? Stand on the sidewalk waiting? Go up to a house and hope it's the right one? And what if it isn't? So instead you sit in the car and stare down this tree-lined street full of historic homes and wait, hoping someone will finally come along that you recognize.

- Tate Hall. Named for Lee H. Tate, a graduate who died in World War I. It is located on Conley Avenue, adjacent to Jesse Hall on the University of Missouri campus. The building has been recently renovated. Before Tate Hall housed the English department[8] it was once home to the school of law.[9]
- Intersection of Stewart Road and Providence Road. If driving down Providence, on the right at this intersection is the entrance to the Katy Trail.[10]

---

Then later at the gathering when you tell this story and explain your worry, your fear of accidentally showing up unannounced at a stranger's home, someone will interrupt you.

"Oh you *can't* be serious," she'll respond.

8. Your office is in the basement of this building. You remember how before classes had started you'd gone to find it. You stopped and took in a deep breath when you saw the sign with your name. It was something as simple as your name typed on a piece paper letting you know that this space was yours. It didn't matter that the desk would be shared with another person, that your office space was in the back of the room in the very farthest corner. What mattered to you then was that you could look at this paper, see your name, and know how far you'd come.

9. In 1936, an African American man named Lloyd Gaines applied for admission to the law school. At the time of his application, only whites were admitted to the university. Gaines applied and received interest from admissions, but after the university learned of Gaines' race from his transcripts he was denied admission. In response Gaines sued the university, claiming that his right to "equal protection of the laws" under the Fourteenth Amendment had been violated. The United States Supreme Court ruled in Gaines' favor, upholding that the school either had to provide a separate law school or admit blacks to the university.

Gaines disappeared on March 19, 1939, a year after his landmark case. He left his apartment to buy postage stamps, or so he told a friend, and then vanished. He was twenty-eight years old, the same age you were when you moved here to start this program.

10. An old rail bridge used to be here but it's now gone. Once a man was lynched on that bridge. His name was James T. Scott. He was a janitor working at the MU medical school when he was accused and arrested for raping the white

- Faurot Field. Named in honor of longtime coach Don Faurot. Faurot Field is located at Memorial Stadium. It's the home field for the Missouri Tigers,[11] the University of Missouri's football team where Gary Pinkel is the head coach.
- Traditions Plaza. Traditions Plaza is located in the heart of campus on the Carnahan Quadrangle.[12] Traditions Plaza is also across

---

daughter of an MU German professor, Hermann Almstedt. While Scott was in jail a mob broke in, took him from his cell, and dragged him to this bridge where he was lynched.

Even now, there is no sign, no official marking of remembrance.

11. You're in a student computer lab in another campus building where you teach. You're trying to print out an assignment for your class and you're doing it here because you are avoiding your office, avoiding the conversations from your cohort about the protests, avoiding their white guilt frustrations and concerns, avoiding their questions asking you for your black perspective. You're alone in this lab, or you were until you hear another person behind you come in.

"It's all such a disaster. I don't know why the football players were protesting in the first place. Like why they even had to get involved. It's not their job to get involved," a woman says to someone on her phone. She's young, a student most likely, and she comes in and sits at a nearby table.

"It wasn't all the football players," she says. "I wish everyone would realize that. It was just those—"

She stops, swallows. She looks over at you, has suddenly become aware of your presence. *Go ahead and say it,* you think. *Just fucking say it.*

"Let me call you back," she tells the person on the other line, then she gets back up and leaves.

12. A well-known writer comes to visit. You sit in a room with your cohort as this writer says what you wish you had the nerve to say—she talks about academic racism, the lack of diversity across the board, the microaggressions students of color often face, and the biases and stereotypes others who, despite believing themselves to be better, often perpetuate.

Across from you another minority student sits. *"Yes,"* she softly says with each statement made, and it becomes clear to both of you who this writer is addressing, but it is only clear to the two of you.

from Jesse Hall along Conley Avenue. The plaza was created in
honor of MU's landmark 175th anniversary.

- Gateway Hall. Its name "combines the historic[13] past with MU
  as the first established university west of the Mississippi." The
  building is newly constructed and is located on the southeast side
  of campus.

- Top Ten Wines. It is, according to their website, "one of Columbia's most prominent wine venues, occupying a unique niche for

---

What you've noticed lately in the time since the protests is that there has been
a disassociation between the response and its cause. *We have moved on from this stain*
is the underlying consensus. Already, there is a sense of finality to the problem,
but you are in a room in which you are one of a handful of minorities. When
you look out at everyone else all you can see is another problem, one of many,
and none of which anyone seems to want to face.

After this writer has finished one of them points to the window. "Out there
was where the protests happened," she says. "If you look really close you can kind
of see the plaza." You are struck by this action, in how she begins to talk about
what had happened. Already, the events have become conversational fodder for
tourists. It makes you wonder if in the future the university will do this as well.
If in five years or ten it will be included in the campus tours. How much will be
mentioned? How much, you wonder, will be erased?

13. The poop swastika. For months it'll be all anyone talks about—where it was,
who saw it, whether it existed or was completely fabricated. Even your friend will
ask, *well how do we know since there's not a photo?* And you'll have to remind her that
there is, that there's a police report, that it's all easily accessible online. Never
mind that this is not the only racist incident to have happened. Never mind that
there is a history of reports of students being called slurs and of veiled threats on
social media. Never mind about the cotton balls thrown on the lawn of the Black
Culture Center. Never mind because what matters is that for this the doubt has
been cast. It is the question that has come to matter. There is such an infatuation
with the possibility of a falsehood that no one wants to stop and think about the
implications of what it would mean if it were true.

wine enthusiasts in the area."[14] Every Tuesday is known as Tapas Tuesdays where tapas are served with every wine, beer, or sangria purchase.[15]

- Jesse Hall. This is the main administrative building on campus.[16]

---

14. Three days before you have to take your oral exams. Three days and the walls of your apartment are cluttered with notecards push-pinned to corkboard. You've spent the past year reading the canon of African American history and learning the weight of its history, and you are tired of the patterns you see, of the ways in which the past is continuously played out before your eyes. The world around you appears to be falling apart, and so you take a break, get your keys and you are out, out, out—at a bar forgetting, just having a moment, and after a few hours your shoulders relax and you really do forget about the fact that if you were to turn on the television there would be your campus on full display.

15. Then the threat comes. *I'm going to stand my ground tomorrow and shoot every black person I see.* Your students email you screen-capped images. *Some of you are alright. Don't go to campus tomorrow.* You get an email from a friend. You get emails from your department. You get an email from the university.

Fear is like a fever, feel its heat running through your body as you quickly exit the bar and make your way down the street. Fear is what you'll think as you walk to your car. It's late, you're one of the few people out. You do not run because there's a part of you not wanting to overreact. It's a prank, you'll find out later, and even now you are telling yourself that it is just a prank, that no one could ever be serious in such a threat, and yet still you sit in your car unable to start the engine, unable to even move out of fear of being seen.

16. Because it's the main administrative building, the campus's center, if you will, it will be the focal spot for a number of protest marches. Students will chant "Racism Lives Here," as the crowds surrounding them become larger as their path of egress is blocked.

"I can't get by. These fuckers," you hear someone from behind you say. You have left your office and are on your way to class when you become blocked because of the march. You turn and look among the sea of faces for the person belonging to the comment but no one now is talking. Everyone stares straight ahead at the line. They grow impatient the longer it takes.

You close your eyes. You don't want to see the faces of the other students, their barely contained expressions of anger and resentment. You don't want to

Built in 1893 after Academic Hall burned to the ground, the building is one of the major symbols of the University. It is located at
the south end of the David R. Francis Quadrangle, often called
simply "The Quad." Jesse Auditorium, a popular entertainment
venue for touring acts, is located at the east end of the hall.

- Speaker's Circle. Speaker's Circle actually used to be known as
Conley Plaza. Built in 1986, Conley Plaza was to be a concrete
open space framed with seasonal flora from the school's botanical
garden. Later that year, a group of students constructed shantytowns on the nearby quad in protest of the university's 127.5-mil-
lion-dollar investments in companies operating in South Africa
during apartheid. The shantytowns stayed briefly before the university tore them down. The students built them again. For this
act of civil disobedience the students were arrested.

- Eventually, the university would comply and divest their funds
from connections to the apartheid government. In response to
the protests the university president designated Conley Plaza as
the only area on the campus where speakers didn't need to have
permits.[17]

---

be reminded of your own guilt for not joining in, for continuing to stand there
waiting because you are afraid. You are afraid of making yourself known.

It finally quiets down, and when you open your eyes again the crowd has
passed. Students disperse. The moment, this one, is over, and as you look around
you find that you are the only one left.

17. Sometimes you'll catch one of the tours as you walk through this area on your
way to teach a class. "It's one of the few areas in Missouri where you can practice
free speech," one of the guides explains, but another time you hear a guide say
"in the country" instead of "in Missouri" . Both times you want to ask them
what specifically they meant by their statements, but you are late and there's no
time to ask for clarifications.

You remember though how once you had a student meet with you to discuss
a potential paper topic. He wanted to argue that Speaker's Circle wasn't an area
of free speech, not really, because he felt afraid to be able to say what he wanted
without repercussions.

- Memorial Student Union. Memorial Union honors university men who lost their lives in service during World War I. Their names are inscribed on the inside walls of the tower archway. In a tradition dating back to a time when most men wore hats, whenever one walks beneath the archway they are to tip their hat as a sign of respect to their deceased brothers. Every student is also to speak at a whisper under the archway. [18]
- Phi Kappa Psi Fraternity House. The Phi Kappa Psi Fraternity House is the oldest fraternity house on campus. [19] Recognized as "The Grasslands," the house was built in 1878 by George Bingham Rollins, the son of the founder of the University of Missouri.

---

"Well, what do you want to say?" you had asked, and he wouldn't answer.

18. This will be the first building on campus you'll go to. An orientation specifically for minority students with fellowships will be held in this building. You have what's known as the Gus T. Ridgel Fellowship, named after a man who was the first African American to earn a Master's degree at the university. Even though there's no building named after him, a room here has been and one of the meetings is held in it.

This fellowship—you almost didn't want to come here because of it, ashamed as you are to admit it. Despite the honor, you did not want to be labeled the minority with the scholarship.

"Girl, take that money," a family member said when you called and ask her for advice, and so you accepted their offer. "They're still going to see you as black, money or no money, so you might as well take it and move on."

Years later, after you've been called the first slur and the second and then the third, you'll call up an old friend to tell him what happened. "You know," he'll say, "I never thought you should have gone there in the first place."

"Well," you'll say, thinking back to your family member's advice. "They offered me the most money. What else was I supposed to do?"

19. Once known as Grasslands Plantation, there is a campus rumor that the house is haunted.

"Perhaps it's the ghosts of the slaves that worked the land," you'll respond when your students tell you this about the fraternity. "Maybe they're wanting their reckoning."

- The State Historical Society of Missouri. The State Historical
  Society's[20] mission is to "collect, preserve, make available, and pub-

---

20. You've come here one afternoon to look through their archives in an attempt
to find out more about the town's history. You stand at the front desk, fill out the
necessary forms, give the woman working your identification and listen to her
as she goes over the rules. When she's finished she asks you what you're looking
for and you pause, and then for some reason you begin to tell her something else.

"I'm doing research on this senator," you say. "He didn't live in this state
though so I don't know what you'll have, what you'll even be able to access."

"We have databases for newspapers," she tells you. "That might prove useful.
Also census records. What's his name?"

You tell her and she begins typing in the computer. While you wait you look
around the room at the others quietly hunched over their tables looking at the
materials they've requested. In the back corner you recognize another student
from your department but he does not look up to meet your gaze.

You wait, listening as she clicks through several pages, until finally she looks
back at you.

"There's a collection of his papers in Chapel Hill. Your best bet may be though
to go there and look through these."

"Yeah," you tell her, explaining that you know about the papers. "Is there
anything else?"

"It looks like—" she stops, shifting in her seat as she moves closer to the
computer screen. "It looks like he lived here in Missouri for a bit. Did you know
this?"

"What? No, no I didn't."

She tells you that Bedford Brown left North Carolina after his second
bid for senator failed. His son-in-law was John Bullock Clark, a Confederate
congressman of Fayette, MO. "It seems like he moved there and lived with him."

"Do you think if I went to Fayette to their courthouse I could find out where
he specifically he lived? Would they even have anything?"

"Maybe. It's worth a shot. It's not far from here at least."

You thank her and go to one of the computers she'd mentioned. You decide to
look for information about Fayette and learn about Frank Embree. On July 22,
1899, a mob of over a thousand people gathered together to lynch Embree, but
before the crowd hung him he was whipped across his legs and back and chest.

lish materials that enhance research and support learning opportunities in Missouri studies and the history of the Midwest." It's Columbia branch is located on the University of Missouri's campus, housed next door to Ellis Library.

- Strickland Hall. Formerly known as the General Classroom Building, Strickland Hall was constructed in 1969 to house classrooms for the social sciences.[21] In 2007, it was renamed "Arvarh

---

In photographs, he stands straight, his gaze directly ahead. He's naked, and in the photo you can see the gashes on his body, the cuts in his flesh.

You are unable to look at the photo for long before you have to exit the browser and stand, quickly walking out of the room and out of the building, looking down, away, from everyone that you pass by.

21. Your professor has to schedule a make-up class, changing the date to a Friday afternoon in this building. You get there early, beginning your slow climb up four flights of stairs to the room since the elevator will not go to the top floor. You have reached the top and are about to rest when a woman comes out the door. She looks at you and asks where you're going.

"I have a class up here."

"There are no classes up here today."

"Well," and then you explain. She interrupts several times to ask for clarification—*Who is the professor? Oh, I know him. What class you say? What room? Oh, you don't remember, okay what time is your class? Why did he reschedule the date? Why is no one else here with you?*

"I still can't let you in here. This floor gets locked after a certain time and no one without a key can go on."

You tell her okay, that you understand, even though you never asked her in the first place. She's still unsatisfied with leaving you alone so she takes her phone out of her purse.

"I'm just going to call him and ask," she says.

You stare at each other as it rings. The phone goes to voicemail and she leaves a message. She calls again. She calls once more.

"He's not picking up," she says.

E. Strickland Hall" in honor of professor emeritus and former interim Director of the Black Studies Program Arvarh E. Strickland. Dr. Strickland was MU's first tenure-track, black professor.

- Jake's Market, Uncle B's Ice House, Blue and White Cafe, Ginny Taylor's Tavern and Grill, Richardson Shoe Repair, Alvin Coleman's Liquor Store, Green Tree Club, Shook Herndon's Tavern, Phil and William's Barber Shop, Britt's Pool Hall, Merle Slater's Place, Swanson's Plumbing, Miss Vi's Cafe, Coleman's Scrap Yard, Noble's Coal Yard, Lake's Barber Shop, Coleman Cleaners, Green's Funeral Home, Mota Ralph's Chicken and Rib Shack.[22]

---

She sits down on the steps, but the moment she's settled there another student comes and she stands up. "Oh, okay," she says. "I see now." She smiles, nodding at you both, then leaves.

Later, in class, your professor will turn to you and ask about the phone calls. "I don't understand. Why did she care if you were there?"

"I don't know," you'll say, shrugging, hoping he'll move on.

22. These few blocks between Fifth and Sixth streets on both sides of Walnut were once the Sharp End District, an area where during the 1960's black businesses thrived. As part of what was known as "urban renewal" these businesses, along with well over sixty more, were all torn down and are now gone.

- Intersection of S. 9th Street and Conley Avenue. On one side of the crosswalk is Ellis Library.[23] On the other side is Tate Hall.[24]

---

23. After the protests, after you pass your comprehensive exams and you decide you are done with this place, you get up one Sunday morning to go to your office and collect your belongings. You stand on the side of the street waiting to cross when a car comes, a white SUV, speeding around the turn. You hold back and wait for the car to pass, and as it does one of them shouts at you before disappearing on down the road.

You don't need to explain the slur or how it felt to be called it. By now, the hurt should not be surprising, but still you feel the shock from it as you force yourself to cross the street, to continue on what you set out to do.

"You should tell someone," your friend says. "Campus safety. Call them now and tell them."

"What good would it do?" you respond.

"Because people should know this shit keeps happening," she says, "and because people still believe it doesn't."

24. You are back in your office staring at the sign with your name. For a brief moment you think about ripping the sign in two, taking the paper and shredding it to pieces. It would give this act the closure you long for. You reach up and grab it, hold it in your hands. *No*, you think, *no.*

It is the memory of Gaines that makes you tape the sign back. It is what tells you to leave this, because it is a reminder of why you are here. Still though, you can't help but wonder if that's enough. After everything, is it enough you at least have this? Is it enough that you are here?

# If My Heart Should Confess

"I hate this song. It doesn't make any sense."

A friend of mine and I have just had dinner, having gotten together for the first time since she's moved here to Missouri. We're sitting in my parked car talking when I notice the song playing. "I paid for Sirius once I realized there weren't any black stations. I got tired of listening to Taylor Swift all the time, but this isn't much better. It's not even a good rap song."

"Kevin Gates," she says, laughing. "His rap name even sucks! Santana is a better rap name and he isn't even a rapper." She pulls out her phone, searches for the lyrics. She recites them, jokingly imitating a poet persona for fun. After she finishes and both of us have quieted down from laughing, I change the subject.

"I'm sorry I haven't been around," I say, wondering if she can hear my guilt. "After the protests on campus—I just decided I couldn't be around anymore."

"At least everything seems to be settling down for now," she says.

"Have you seen—" I begin before stopping myself, unsure if I should ask.

"He asked about you," she says, answering my question. It was not hard for her to guess who I was referring to since there are only a few of us here in this program.

"What did he say? I haven't talked to him since the start of the semester, since before everything happened. I guess we got into it."

"He just seemed concerned as all. I think he thought you were upset with him."

"Yeah, well," I say, then shrug.

I pause, thinking back to what happened. He was angry at the department's lack of response. It doesn't affect most of them so they don't care, he'd told me. He was frustrated at my cohort, at their apathy. I'm the only one who has to worry about being shot as a black man, he'd said.

For a while he sent out emails forwarded to the entire department, calling on them to put action to their words. Email after email was blasted off, the effect of which causing increasing hostility in response. He eventually decided he wanted to do a boycott, sending out an email to the handful of us in the program.

*You've got to stop this.* I'd finally messaged. *You're just making everyone angry.*

*That's a good thing,* he'd quickly written back.

*Why are you doing this? What about school?*

*This is important,* he answered, then stopped responding to my messages.

His proposed boycott dissipated before it could start, most of us were too occupied with just making it through school to deal with anything else.

I'd thought a lot about his response since. He was so sure, so forceful in what he felt was the right thing to do, even at the risk of potential backlash. In contrast, I remembered my father's response on the night I told him about the protests—*you are there to work, remember? You are there to get your degree and get out, don't lose sight of that goal.* I thought of the ways I had spent my life attempting to erase markers of my blackness until I did not know who I was anymore. I thought of how, even still, the night of the threats I'd sat in my car afraid to start the engine, and I thought of how after, when for a moment the world had seemed to settle down, while walking down the street I was yelled a slur and even then my first instinct was to let it go, to bury it, to ignore the fact that it happened.

You can be good. You can be accommodating. You can make the world comfortable with your blackness as so many of us try to in our daily lives. You can straighten your hair, code-switch, be quiet instead of speaking out, and yet one day you may still find yourself confronted with a group of men, wild-eyed and in a frenzy, who will shout slurs at you, and you will be reminded in the end that in this world it doesn't matter how good you are.

"I should probably get in touch with him," I finally say. In the quiet I reach over and shift to a new station, this one plays D'Angelo. My friend laughs.

"Come on D'Angelo," she says upon hearing the first few verses. "Calling yourself the Black Messiah, as if all of us have forgotten about the time when all anyone cared about was seeing your dick. No one forgot. I still remember."

We both laugh. It's nice sitting in the car with her, the two of us having this moment.

"You know, I feel responsible for encouraging you to come here," I finally admit. "I'm sorry if you've had a hard time."

"It's okay. It hasn't been that bad. I mean, up until now."

"Have you been doing okay?"

She pauses, thinks about my question. "Yeah, someone called me a slur at the beginning of the semester but since things have been fine."

"It happens," I say, and because I am nearing the end of my time here and she's at the beginning, I don't tell her I've been called slurs too, multiple times, and between the both of us it will most likely happen again.

"I'm used to it. Once in school the teacher read out loud *Huck Finn* and kept emphasizing all the slurs. He read them over and over while the rest of class just stared at me. Later, the teacher came up and was like, 'Oh, I didn't realize. This didn't bother you, did it?'"

"Seriously?"

"Must be nice to go through your life like that—offending people and not worrying about it until afterward," she pauses. "It doesn't matter; they're just words. I tried telling my parents about it, what with it and then with the protests, and they didn't understand."

"I know what you mean. My father went to school the year after Wilmington Ten," I say, remembering the story of what happened. In February of 1971 in Wilmington, NC tensions over school desegregation had reached a breaking point. Four days of violence rocked the town, resulting in two deaths and the firebombing of a white-owned store. The National Guard had to come in to restore the peace. The Wilmington Ten were a group of students convicted of arson and conspiracy to fire upon firemen and police officers. They were sentenced to 282 years in prison. After their sentencing, a movement formed in the state demanding their freedom.

"So it's like," I say, continuing. "I call my father up sometimes and I'll say—well, so and so said this, or this happened, and he'll be like, 'so what's the problem? Your *feelings* were hurt? Is that why you're calling?'"

"It's the price of admission for being here," she says, and I nod.

"You know, I'm thinking about writing about all this—a bunch of essays about race." I then explain about my family, about their history. I tell her I'm thinking of going to Louisiana, of visiting the Whitney Museum, the first plantation dedicated to the memory of slavery. "My ancestors were all on tobacco plantations, not so much cotton or sugar like in the Deep South, but I still feel as if I have to go and see the ones there, especially the Whitney. Who knows if anything will come from it but I'm gonna go. The time's there, better make use before it's gone."

"I went to a lot of them for my novel," she tells me. "We went to one that had an intact slave cabin and it was so hot I almost passed out, but I thought—this was how it was, they were working in this heat, and so I pulled myself together."

"Those plantations are something else."

"I know, so many columns."

"That Greek Revival architecture."

"All built on the backs of slaves."

"I've never talked about race before," I suddenly say, thinking about this book and my hesitancy to write it. "I always thought if I avoided it maybe others wouldn't see me as different."

It has taken me years to get to this confession, it has taken me most of my life. Saying it out loud feels as if I am reaching closer, that I am slowly reclaiming back my sense of self.

"People are going to see you that way though. No matter what they want to pretend."

She has already gotten to a place I am still struggling to reach. I don't respond, don't know how to, and for the first time during our evening we both have settled into silence.

"Oh, here we go." I motion to the new song on the radio. Beyoncé's "Formation" has just started playing. "I used to be so critical of her, but now I don't know what to think. What about you? Do you think she's being authentic with this album? That her video is pandering?"

"I don't know. Maybe. I'm not sure how much it matters though."

I don't know this answer either, but what I wonder is how I would have felt had I heard this when I was younger—to witness such an affirmation of blackness, and even though my heart skips a moment, a tinge of nervousness, of insecurity from others around us passing by, I roll the windows down anyway, and let the music fill the air.

# As For Me And My House

To get there, you must first cross the Gramercy Bridge, also known as the Veterans Memorial Bridge, which links St. James Parish with the St. John the Baptist Parish. It is a cantilever bridge, the sixth longest one in the world, constructed to replace the ferry system that caused the 1976 accident that killed 78 people. As I drive along Louisiana State Highway 3213 to cross the bridge, there is a slight incline and I try to focus ahead and not on the steel beams keeping me from drowning in the Mississippi below. I've never been a fan of bridges and it is all I can do to keep the shaking of my hands from affecting my steering. My car slows as it hits the bridge's descent, and in the distance I can see the miles and miles of sugar fields. It is early May, several months from grinding season, and the familiar stalks are not yet seen, but I am still able to recognize the fields.

After the bridge I have to make a turn onto LA-18, otherwise known as River Road, this 70-mile stretch between Baton Rouge and New Orleans that parallels the Mississippi. River Road will take me to Vacherie, an unincorporated community, one of the several that exist here. This area consists not of cities or towns but of communities such as Vacherie, and it does not take me long to get there. I drive further still on River Road, passing the St. Joseph Plantation where, if it was autumn I'd be able to go on their "Creole Mourning Tour." Nearby is also the Laura Plantation where a brochure tells me the original Br'er Rabbit folktales were recorded. After St. Joseph and near the Laura, just before River Road curves, leading to residential properties, there is one last plantation—Oak Alley, and Oak Alley is one of two I have traveled here to see.

I have always loved architecture, the way and shape of houses and the materials used to construct them. This fascination I think comes from my father. He sells real estate, but even before then he used to take me on drives to different neighborhoods so we could gaze upon the homes and imagine the lives lived inside of them. It's a practice he still continues because of his job but the difference now is that when I come home to visit and we pass a house for sale or one recently built, he'll ask if I want to see inside, and I'll say yes. I always say yes, and then we'll go.

When my father was a child his own house burned down, causing him and his brothers and sisters to be split up among the other family members who could take them in. It is not something he talks much about but I've thought about it often on these trips as he pointed out to me how it's always the kitchen that sells the house. I've learned from him to look beyond the easy fixes—the personal preferences when it comes to aesthetics, for instance, because "paint is cheap and you're buying the house not the home," as he often would remind me when I commented on the owner's taste in furniture or the color scheme. My father would note the crown molding in one or whether the floors were actual hardwood or laminate in another. He's observant, taking note of every detail, every feature, as if he was always the one buying. He's American dreaming, and he would bring me on those trips because he wanted me to dream with him too.

You may not know the name of Oak Alley but you've seen images of its plantation before. The plantation has been the site for the films *Interview with the Vampire* and *Primary Colors*, along with a string of made-for-tv movies. As I wait for the next tour to start, I notice a brochure that boasts the productions filmed in part or entirely on the location.

At Oak Alley a plantation bell, once the communication system for governing slaves on the plantation, is now used to signal the beginning of guided tours. When I hear the bell I go to the entrance of the Big House with the rest of the crowd.

This tour, like most, if not all in the South, focuses on the Big House, otherwise known as the plantation owner's home. In Louisiana, these owners were sugar cane farmers, and they were wealthy. They were considered to be antebellum royalty, and when we think of the idea of the Old South with its Southern belles and aristocratic planters, it is images of these plantations that come to mind.

Evie, my tour guide, is dressed in period costume. She wears a plaid hoop skirt with a thick black belt buckled around her slim waist. Her hair is pulled back in a bun. She corrals us all in a dining room of the Big House as she begins to talk about the Roman family of Oak Alley. I am the only black person and even though I've had the past hour to try and settle into the realization that I would most likely be the only black person I see, it's a different feeling altogether standing there with all of us measuring each other up. While Evie talks others snap photos of the room's interior. I shift my position toward the back near one of the framed portraits.

On the tour, there is no talk of slavery, so while Evie tells us of how Jacques Telesphore Roman built Oak Alley for his wife Celina, she doesn't mention the slave labor it took to construct it. The one and only reference to a slave is when Evie explains about the punkah, a large wooden fan suspended from the ceiling, and how it was a slave's job, usually a child's, to pull a cord attached to it so that a gentle breeze could blow on the guests to keep them cool as they ate.

What Evie does talk about is the Romans. Evie entwines stories of the Roman family with descriptions of the house and its furnishings. We walk up the creaking steps to the bedrooms, and Evie tells us of how after her husband Jacques died Celina was so stricken with grief she could no longer sleep in their shared bedroom.

"Isn't it all just so beautiful?" a woman leans in and whispers to me as we're gathered in the hall. "Can you imagine living during this period?"

"No, I don't think so."

The woman, annoyed by my response, moves away to view another one of the rooms.

I must admit though, Oak Alley is beautiful. I'd be lying if toward the end of the tour, I said I didn't almost gasp along with the others when Evie opened the front veranda doors to the image of what's known as the "Alley of the Oaks." The Alley of the Oaks consists of two rows of

300-year-old Virginia Live Oaks that lead to the Mississippi River. After the tour, people crowd outside to take pictures, to pose with the image of these oaks in the background, and I'm not sure I blame them for doing so.

Evie informs us she has to leave to start the next tour and I am left to look out at the oaks with their limbs twisting towards the sky. I stare out at them and it is difficult not to think of *Beloved's* Sethe and her own shame for remembering the beauty of the trees rather than the boys who hung from them.

Like my father, my mother would also take me on drives. On our way home from the store she'd sometimes go a different route to another neighborhood, slowing the car each time when she saw groupings of apartments.

"What do you think about those?" she'd ask, noting a complex.

I would look at the area and smugly grimace. "Those are apartments."

"Well, what if we moved into one of those instead? What if it was just you and me in an apartment somewhere? Would that be so bad?"

"Yes it would. They're not the same. Why does it matter anyway? We have our house."

"Yes, we do," she'd say, and sigh.

I did not realize it then, did not understand the meaning behind her question, at least not fully. After the divorce, my mother struggled. She had health problems, lupus and a bad heart, and the mounting debt from medical bills. Throughout my childhood she also struggled to find stable income with health insurance. Most of the jobs I remember—she was a cashier at a gas station Taco Bell, moonlighted at a front desk at a Days Inn, worked as a part-time security guard—were not enough to cover the expenses of raising a child alone.

She was asking for a different life, one I didn't want, and so we stayed in the house we couldn't afford to live in because it was the idea of it, of stability and progress and the American dream, that mattered.

In the Oak Alley gift shop there are Southern treats galore. Bourbon and mint julep balls. Caramels. Glass jars of moonshine. Creole pecans, pralines, and kettle corn. A man wearing a chef hat and a blue and white apron roasts pralines in a pan. The aroma of heated butter and sugar wafts through the air.

At the register, a woman asks if I'd like a sample of their pecan liqueur. She tells me the story about the slave gardener Antoine who was the first to successfully graft pecan trees. I take one of the tiny paper cups and sip the sample, almost gagging on its sweetness. "Too sweet for you?" she says, interrupting her own story, and offers up her hand to take my crumpled cup.

There is even a penny machine. I can't resist this, knowing a friend of mine will want one, and so I dig in my purse searching for enough money to put in the machine. I crank the lever, turning, as the machine flattens and presses the design into my penny. When finished, it clinks down into the slot for me to take. My fingers rub over the indentation.

I repeat the process once more, making another penny to keep.

Besides the gift shop, outside there's a "Spirits Bar" and a restaurant serving Creole fare. Nearby the slave quarters, a grouping of century-old cottages can be rented out for the night. It is early in the day still, the swampy heat I'd imagined has not yet come, and right now a cool breeze blows to stifle any sweat. If one so chooses, they can go to the back of the Big House and purchase mint juleps or bourbon lemonades for sale. Wrought iron chairs have been planted around the house's perimeter and I watch as visitors relax in them with their drinks.

Pretend is what they're offering here. Pretend is the name of the game. The Roman family, like the many others who owned these plantations, were wealthy and they had power. They were the planter aristocracy of the South, but they represented only a few of the time who were. Historians have usually granted planter status to those who owned twenty slaves or more. In 1860, when plantation agriculture reached its peak, there were roughly 46,000 plantations, the greatest proportion of these consisting of estates with 20 to 30 slaves. The majority of Southerners were yeoman farmers. If they did own slaves, they were usually one or two. Yet, these farmers looked up to the planter aristocracy with admiration. They wanted what they had and believed they could achieve it.

We live in a world where income equality continues to rise, where most of us have neither wealth nor power, but you can come here and pretend. You can come and sip bourbon lemonades on a Big House porch, sleep in a cottage with views of the once-homes of slaves. You can come here and romanticize a life that never was yours, never would have been yours, but for a moment you can believe it could have been. People come here to have the replication of an experience that was, even then, never within their reach.

Not far from Oak Alley, on the west bank of the Mississippi, is the rural community known as Wallace. On the way to Wallace a truck tails me from behind, pushing me to go faster down the road. It is just the two of us and I slow, hoping he'll pass, but he is relentless in his refusal to back down. He honks his horn, a series of loud spurts that puts me on edge. I force myself to try not to look for him in the rearview mirror but I do it anyway.

I end up missing my stop and have to drive several miles along the winding LA-18 before I can turn around. The whole while the man behind me continues to honk as he edges closer to the rear of my car. I turn off the road, relieved, and the truck passes me. The driver gives me the finger as he disappears down the road.

Circling back, I pass the site of the Evergreen Plantation, one of the most complete plantations in the South. You are probably familiar with the image of its Big House, with its Greek Revival style columns and its two curved front staircases. Quentin Tarantino's *Django Unchained* was filmed at this plantation.

I have not come for this one or for the several others that are available for tours in this area. Not for the Houmas House or the San Francisco. Not the Laura or the Destrehan. There are so many, more even than these I've listed, and if I could I'd go to them all—if I had the time and if I could afford it—I would go and see all the ways in which they have chosen to narrate history. To see what they've included and what, more importantly, they've decided to leave out, but because of time I can only visit one more—the Whitney, the first and only museum in the United States dedicated to the memory of slavery.

A few years ago my father bought his dream house. "I'm going to get the house I want before I die," he told me as he carted me along to look. Meanwhile, he scrimped and saved so that when he finally found it, he'd have enough put away to buy it.

The house my father eventually bought is two floors with six bedrooms and four bathrooms. The master bedroom on the second floor opens up to a veranda with a view of the street. Sometimes, my father will take his camp gear and sleep out there.

When I'm not here to visit my father closes off the spare bedrooms. He is rarely downstairs except when he needs to be in the kitchen. Most of his time is spent between his own bedroom and what's called a "bonus room" which he's turned into a movie room, complete with a popcorn machine, a candy machine, and a mini-fridge.

I told a friend of mine all of this once. I'd just come over to see her new apartment and we were sitting in her bedroom. She was struggling to find a place for all her belongings. She had boxes and boxes of clothes— they had filled up her walk-in closet and filled an additional rolling closet and a bureau and still there was more.

"Your father lives alone in a house with six bedrooms? Why does he need so many?"

"Seriously?" I'd said, looking around. "Because he can afford it and because it's what he always wanted. Besides, do you really need so many clothes?"

"Good point," she said, shrugging.

The house I grew up in was a brick ranch-style home, the third one on a cul-de-sac. Shortly after my father bought it, he planted two Dogwood trees in the front yard. He cultivated a rose garden next to the front porch as a gift for my mother.

As part of their divorce settlement, my mother and I were allowed to stay in the house until I turned eighteen. Afterward, the house was sold and my mother moved an hour away to be closer to work.

"I don't know why she left," my father used to always ask. "She could have stayed in the house and I would have made the mortgage payments. She never had to leave."

"That's not how she always made it seem."

"Well," he trailed off, not wanting to finish. He did not want to talk badly about my mother now that she's gone, now that she's unable to clarify her version of the past.

"She probably didn't want to stay in it anyway. The house was falling apart," I said, letting him off the hook.

"Yeah, man that house had some problems," my father then said, laughing. "The builders really cut corners with its construction. It was the first house I bought though."

My father has the same nostalgia that I carry when I remember it, nostalgia that blinds me from remembering the settling foundation, the cracks in the walls and the broken chimney. I don't think about the back-yard deck that needed new paint or the piles of molding firewood that had attracted termites. We had a sinkhole in our backyard and every year despite our efforts it gained in depth and scope, and every time my father brings it up I still smile at the memory.

"I have to make a disclaimer of sorts," Ali, our tour guide, tells the crowd. Ali wears a t-shirt and khaki shorts, his dreads are pulled into a ponytail that falls down the length of his back. His voice is cheery and buoyant as he herds us together. "On this tour you'll get to see the Big House but that's not going to be the focus. We're telling a different story here. I'm not going to glorify the Haydel family to you. I'm going to talk about the exploitation of the people who built this place and gave the Haydels their wealth."

The crowd nods in response. Satisfied, Ali tells us our first stop is the Antioch Baptist church. On our way there, we pass a large bell and he explains that this is an antique church bell meant to honor the lives of slaves. Whenever we see one he asks for us to ring it, and immediately someone from the crowd goes up and pushes. Its loud clang reverberates around us and I think of the plantation bell I saw earlier, reminded of how they were used to call.

The tour takes over two hours. Ali is unforgiving in his portrayals of the owners, in his retelling of history. He tells us about Jean Jacques Haydel's wife, Marcellin. Because Marcellin couldn't have children, she kept a girl slave named Anna as a pet. The sun bears down, the heat of the day in full swing, as we walk through the series of memorials and listen.

"Imagine grinding season," Ali says. "There was the slave saying, 'can to can't,' meaning working from 'can see' in the morning to 'can't see' at night. You know, maybe they'd get a break at noon for a meal, the slave bell call letting to know it's time, but mostly the day was work, from dawn to dusk and during grinding season even longer."

"Can you see it?" he asks, and I imagine a field burning. Fire set to flame the land. The field must be burned before it can be harvested. Smoke so thick some slaves get lost in it, their bodies left to burn.

Cane knives—long, with a wide blade to strike through the sharp leaves covering the field. Imagine the sugar stalks seven, eight, nine, almost ten feet tall with leaves sharp enough to cut the skin, leaving a trail of blood. Sugar born of blood will taste of blood from the bodies of those who died in the fields. From the fire, or from those not quick enough to dodge the blade swooping down to cut the stalks, or those whose bodies have given out from heat exhaustion or sickness. Imagine the blood gliding down the backs of those who keep going, the blood mixing with sweat to soil the earth.

As we walk, Ali mentions the 1811 German Coast Uprising. A man named Charles Deslondes, a former slave driver, led one of the largest slave revolts ever recorded. Armed with the machetes they'd used to cut sugar cane, Deslondes, along with five hundred other slaves, invaded the Big House mansions as they traveled along River Road towards New Orleans. The revolt was swiftly and brutally put down. Those that were captured were dismembered, their heads cut off and put on spikes to decorate the German coast. It was a lesson for all the other slaves to see, for them to know that this was what awaited if anyone tried to choose a different fate.

Ali then leads us to a memorial for all the slave children who died before the age of three. He asks us to go through the over two thousand listings, to take note of how most have no names. *Little negro boy*, one reads. *A negro boy, a mulatto corpse of a little slave.* That is what I notice. One after the other the listings go—*corpse of a little slave, corpse of a little slave, corpse of a little slave.* Not even names, only a description of their bodies left to give remembrance.

Ali is earnest in the telling of these stories, and at times his emotion feels heavy-handed, but I suspect he has to be. Here there is the "Plantation Parade," after all, the series of plantation tours with their own spin on the past, with most of them giving only a cursory look to the exploitation that provided the plantation's existence. Ali has to tell this story because if he didn't no one else would.

He'd explained earlier that he and his family are descendants of the slaves and sharecroppers who worked this land, and how the church we saw earlier was the same one his grandparents went to. I watch him as he tells these stories, and there are moments when I can hear his voice begin to crack, and I can't help but think of what it must mean to retell these stories over and over again.

Ali takes us along the rows of sugar kettles while explaining about the danger of the sugar mills. "They died from heat exhaustion. From strokes. They died from burns and infections—"

"Was there any hope at all?" a woman interrupts. Her cheeks are flushed red and she has a strained expression across her face.

Ali pauses, thinks a minute about her question. "Well, I'd like to think there was. I mean, there's always hope, isn't there?"

Ali's response makes me think of all the ways in which we took control of our lives—the rebellions we formed in our fight for freedom, the hush harbors where we took their religion and made it our own, and the maroon colonies we escaped to. It was hope that moved us forward despite the world trying to force us back.

"We all owe society a reparation of some kind," Ali says, finishing the tour. Everyone claps, and one by one they all go up to shake his hand. He walks us back to the gift shop where we first met and then says goodbye.

Inside now I have a chance to look around. There is no penny machine here. No pecan liquors or jars of moonshine for sale. No kitschy souvenirs or memorabilia. Mostly, what's here are books—the slave narratives of Harriet Jacobs, Solomon Northup, Frederick Douglass and the neo-slave narratives of Toni Morrison's *Beloved,* Octavia Butler's *Kindred,* and Edward P. Jones's *The Known World.* While glancing at the books on display, I look up and am struck by the décor on one of the walls. It is cluttered with an array of post-it notes. I walk closer, see that each one is in response to a question—*"What did this tour mean to you?"*

I go and sit down at the wooden benches near the entrance. I'm tired, between the heat and the walking I need a few moments of air-conditioned rest.

A black woman comes up and sits down next to me. She smiles in my direction, then notices my lanyard. "You going on the tour?"

"I've already done it."

"Oh, how was it? Was it good?"

"Yes," I say, knowing this answer is not enough, but she simply nods.

Others begin to gather. I should go, but I continue sitting a few minutes longer, watching them all wait anxiously in silence. I pull my lanyard off though to stick in my purse, and as I do I notice my hands, tanned a deep brown from the midday sun.

Back outside of the Whitney, I have to stop a moment because the pain in my feet has become unbearable. I look down and see that the gravel has cut through the thin material of my soles and the blisters on my heel are showing through.

My phone rings. It's my father calling, most likely to ask me about my trip. "Did you make it there okay?" he asks as soon as he hears my voice.

"Yeah, I'm here," I tell him.

"Good, good," he says. "How long are you staying?"

"Not long, I'm about to drive back now."

"Wow, so a short visit," he says. This is how our conversations go—terse and static because neither of us has ever learned to talk to the other.

"Well, with me here I'm just coming from this house I've been working on and I'm on my way home. Let me tell you it's been a job."

For the past several months my father has been renovating a house that belonged to his sister who died over a year ago. The house is falling into disrepair, and rather than deal with trying to sell it themselves, my father bought the rest of the family out. His plan is to fix the house up himself, to put in new carpet and cabinetry, a new heating system, paint, and then resell it in the hope of making of profit.

"How's it going?"

"Well, you know, I think it's almost done," he says. "When you come to visit I'll take you to see."

He then starts on one of his digressions, this time telling me about the amount of foreclosures happening in his hometown. Families, most of them black, can't make the payments on their homes anymore and are losing them at a rapid pace. He tells a story about how one of the homes, a foreclosure, was bought for thirty thousand and then sold for three times as much.

"Families were given loans they couldn't afford to begin with, with rising interest rates, and now they can't keep up with the payments. It's a shame. They're really making money off my people," he says, "but that's always been the story."

*That's always been the story.* Is it too much to say that I want our lives to have a different story? Perhaps it is too much to ask for this, like I wonder if it is even possible for us to have new stories unburdened by the history of slavery. I once believed there could be, that I could write them, and yet I am here. I am here because my family came from slaves, of those belonging to former state senator by the name of Bedford Brown. While there are no tours of his plantation it is listed in the National Registry of Historic Homes. It is the tobacco fields of North Carolina that have been my family's story. My ancestors never worked on sugar fields. To my knowledge, I have no stories of Louisiana history embedded in my past, but when I look out and see the church it finally becomes clear to me why I am here and why I've come. This is not my history, my story, and yet it is. It is my story and it is yours because we are all stained with this past. My family was not slaves to these owners but they still were slaves. They did not die on these fields but they died on others. All of the actions of our ancestors are entangled in the shaping of this country, in who we are and what we've come to believe and understand about ourselves.

My father quiets. I tell him I have to go, that I still have the long drive back, and after I hang up the phone I think about taking another photo but the surrounding gate of the Whitney has blocked most of the view. If I strain my neck a little I can see the top of the church from where the tour started. I hold my phone up in the air to take a picture of the steeple, one last photo before I'm gone. As I make the shot, I can hear in the distance the sound of the bell, another tour beginning, and I know that it is time.

# And For By Grace

For my mother's family Sunday tradition meant Sunday prayer. For the first meal and the last they would gather together, link hands, and say a series of prayers—the Shepherd's Psalm, The Lord's Prayer, and everyone's own selected Bible verse. Her father, like many of the men in the family, was a preacher and this practice I assume came from him.

After my mother was married and had started a family of her own, she stopped doing the prayers except for the few times she would carry me back to North Carolina. Our visits home were rare, every other year at most, and because of the distance and the amount of time we were gone, our return always held a certain significance. Out of all the family my mother was the one who left. While a teenager she'd taken out a map of the state and circled colleges as far away as she could go. She picked one, and during her first year there she met a future army man, married him, and then moved even farther away. "I wasn't going back there," she used to tell me whenever I asked her about this time in her life. "I would have done anything to get away."

I watched her as she shifted in her seat, her anxiety becoming more visible as we got closer. "You should start memorizing a verse now," she said during our drive. "Don't embarrass me."

Her father, a man I never knew, had long since died, but my grandmother had remarried another who was also a preacher, a man who could recite the entire Bible by heart.

"What kind of verse should I pick?" I asked, taking out my own Bible and flipping through the pages. I glanced at all the highlighted sections

I'd marked from previous Sunday scriptures as I tried to find something
that would work.

"I don't know, just pick one," she'd sharply reply.

A painting hung on the wall of my grandmother's kitchen where we
gathered for prayers. The painting depicted a white-bearded man who sat
at his own kitchen table. He was hunched over the table's edge, his hands
clasped together and placed in front of his forehead. His eyes were closed.
He prayed.

On the table in front of him was a loaf of bread, a slice of it already
having been cut, most likely from a previous meal. Nearby was a metal
bowl of possibly soup or oatmeal to go with his bread along with a book,
which one would assume at first to be a Bible, but was actually a dictionary.
Next to this a knife laid flat.

A loaf of bread, a bowl of soup, a dictionary. The simplicity of it all
made the image seem somber, poignant. The man prayed for his meager
meal, grateful for what God had given him.

There is a story I must tell you but in order to do so I must tell you of
another one. It is that of Eliza Cook[1]. While a slave to Dr. James H. Cook,
Eliza gave birth to seven of his children. After slavery ended, James Cook's
wife wanted Eliza gone. Perhaps she was full of shame for her husband's
indiscretions, or maybe it was jealousy, or spite. Whatever the reason, she
demanded her husband force Eliza out of the shack where she lived on his
plantation. Cook submitted to his wife and Eliza, a woman who found
herself with nowhere to live, nowhere to go, and with seven children to
feed, turned to the Freedmen's Bureau.

In North Carolina, the bastardy laws required every unmarried
woman with a child to name the father within three years of the birth of
the child. The law also required fathers to support their illegitimate children or face imprisonment. In Eliza's case, she'd been enslaved during her

---

1. The story of Eliza Cook comes from *Labor of Innocents: Forced Apprenticeship in
North Carolina, 1719-1919* by Karin Lorene Zipf.

children's infancy and was unable to testify to their parentage. She argued for a new law to be made that would address situations like hers—women who'd been enslaved but now were free and who, according to the Civil Rights Act of 1866, should be entitled to the same rights as white women. With the help of the Freedmen's Bureau Eliza took James Cook to court to force him to support her and all of his children.

Within my family there's been a story handed down through the generations. It's of a black woman named Leanna Brown who, like Eliza, had a relationship with a white man. The relationship produced two, possibly three children. In the census records for 1880, she is listed with these children on a nearby farm to his property. On the census, each of the children carries her last name, but somewhere between then and now something peculiar happens. The surname, at least for one of them, the boy, was changed to that of his father.

Eliza's case brings forward the possibility that like her, Leanna did take the father of her children to court in the hope he would acknowledge them. Like Eliza, it is possible she showed a sense of agency during a time the world wanted her to have none, and so it is possible that maybe he did relent and claim them.

At least, this is what I start to think, but then I remember the rest of Eliza's story. The court argued that the Civil Rights Act didn't apply to her situation and thereby didn't fall under the jurisdiction of the U.S. District Court. They refused to hear her case. Cook, having won, evicted Eliza and the children from his plantation and they were left dependent upon the Freedmen's Bureau to survive.

My grandmother would eventually give the painting to my mother as a gift, but my mother didn't want it so she threw it away without telling her.

"The picture depressed me," she said afterward. "I couldn't look at it. I wish now though I'd kept the thing. It could have been worth something."

The name of the painting is called *Grace* and was actually originally a photograph taken by Eric Enstrom. After the photograph was developed and printed, Enstrom's daughter began hand-painting copies in oils and selling them in her shop. Travelers stopping in the town of Coleraine, Minnesota saw the framed picture through the studio window and were taken with the image. One after the other got sold and the picture's popularity increased. In 2002 the image became Minnesota's official state photograph. Eventually *Grace* became one of the most reproduced religious images in the country. It is in homes all across the country—above dining tables, on the living room walls, small copies placed in wallets and purses. What my mother hoped was rare, significant, was just a copy of a copy, reproduced hundreds, if not thousands of times.

No matter how much I practiced, halfway through the Sunday prayers I'd falter, forgetting the rest of the words. I'd mumble through the rhythm hoping no one would notice, then we'd finish and get to the verse and by then I couldn't remember which one I'd picked. I'd stall, letting the others go, hoping during that span of time I would remember, but it would come to me and I would open my mouth to find I had no words to say.

"Jesus wept," my grandmother whispered. "Just say Jesus wept."

*Jesus wept.* The shortest verse in the Bible, said by Jesus after seeing Lazarus' sister's grief. Even though Jesus had come to raise Lazarus from the dead and there was no reason for his tears, he bore witness to Mary's sorrow and was moved by it. Her pain brought on his own.

My grandmother said the verse again, urging me to repeat after her, but my mother interrupted. "No," she said, gripping my hand tight. "She has her own verse. She can say it. Hurry up now so we can eat."

Unrelenting, my mother would make me stand there until I said it, and the rest of the family would patiently wait, and so they all stood firm, silently still. I swallowed hard, glanced up at the familiar painting, and then somehow I remembered.

"For it is by grace—for it is by grace you have been saved," I began.

The hymn "Amazing Grace" was written by a white British man by the name of John Newton. Newton was a slave trader. The song was inspired from an experience Newton had while sailing his slave ship back home. During the night they'd passed through a violent storm and Newton had woken to find his ship filling with water. He prayed to God for a "great deliverance" to save him and his ship from the ocean's depths. His deliverance came and Newton wrote the first words to his hymn from the experience.

Newton renounced slavery five years before the publication of "Amazing Grace." He became an evangelical minister, of all things, and the hymn echoes his regrets over his involvement in the slave trade. The "Amazing Grace" spoken of alludes to God's forgiveness of Newton's sins. "I once was lost, but now I am found," the first verse of the hymn goes. "Was blind, but *now* I see."

During the eulogy for Clementa Pinckney there was a point where President Obama paused, then he bowed his head. A brief silence followed, and as he lifted his head back up he began to croon the first few words of "Amazing Grace." The crowd roared in response. Never mind that later he would be criticized for using a hymn written to describe God's forgiveness for a man's participation in the slave trade. No one thought of this now, instead the audience stood. They clapped their feet and cheered as he sang to them the well-known hymn. In a moment of black pain it was a call to rise up. It was a balm meant to soothe a wound open for far too long. It was a way of saying—we will get through this, together we will come together and heal in the ways we've always done. We will exhibit God's grace and get through and, and perhaps, forgive.

"What is the thing you couldn't forgive?" my mother asked me once. "Like, how far do you believe forgiveness goes for a person? Because I think it's not the same for everyone."

We'd gone out for dinner, one of the few times in my memory when she had a little money to afford it. The question had come out of nowhere, and I supposed she asked it as a personal musing and had not meant for me to respond.

"Are you talking about dad? For leaving? For the divorce?"

"What? No, I'm not talking about your father."

"Who then? *Your* father? Is this about him?"

I'd regretted asking her the moment I said it. She was always dodgy about telling me about her father, and the few details I knew were when she'd let her guard down. I'd hoped that maybe this time she'd finally tell me everything. I settled back in the booth and waited for her to say the words.

"Just forget it," she answered, then took a long sip of her coke before telling me she didn't want to talk anymore.

A few weeks earlier, I'd sat on the opposite side of the bathroom door listening to my mother grimace in pain. "Are you okay? What's wrong? Should I do something?"

"I am going to have my tubes tied," I heard her say to herself. "No, I am going to have them taken out and *burned*."

It'll be years before I'm able to thread this story together, before I fully understand the context of these events and their relationship to each other, and when I do I will be angry at everyone—at my father for leaving, at the man who would not leave his wife, and at my mother for all of what she never said.

Charles Wilden is the name of the man in the *Grace* photograph. Wilden was an itinerant salesman, a peddler who sold foot-scrapers. One day Wilden ventured upon Enstrom's door as he was preparing a portfolio of his images to take with him to a convention. It was Wilden's "kind face" that made Enstrom ask if he could take his picture. Enstrom was the one who told him to pose, to clasp his hands and bow his head, among the intentionally placed items on the table.

Not much is known about Wilden. A few years after he posed for the photo, he signed over his rights to the image for five dollars. Stories about him tell not of his piety but of him as a drunk. He was married and divorced. He was a Swedish immigrant, but from where and when no one knows for sure. Where he lived after the photo was taken, what became of his life, and where he died, is a mystery. He is a man who is both famous and unknown.

A study lead by Dr. Rachel Yehuda, director of Mount Sinai's Traumatic Stress Studies Division, found that the effects of intense psychological trauma could be hereditary. In the study, the DNA of Holocaust survivors and their children was examined. They found a pattern to suggest that not only could life experiences like stress have a chemical effect on someone's DNA but also that such an effect could be passed down from one generation to the next.

Even though the study was on Holocaust survivors, I have thought of it when you spoke to me about apologies. I thought of when you gave your call of forgiveness and this is my response—the ready noose hanging from the tree, the bodies plucked from beds in the night, the bodies hung, the bodies lost, the postcards taken of all the mutilated bodies, the collectibles of body parts, the ways bodies have been fetishized—the eyes that would stare and mock what would be admired on the body of another, the eyes that would use their stare as justification for the rape of a body, all these bodies beaten, the bodies shot, the law of three-fifths of a body, the sterilization of bodies, the jumpin' Jim Crow depiction of our bodies, the imprisonment of bodies, the legalized murder of bodies, the systematic oppression of bodies, the tainted water meant to fill the spirit of bodies but poisoned them instead, the shame taught over the body, all the bodies still being silenced, and now the ways in which my body has been changed before it ever even was my body— you apologize, asking for forgiveness, but an apology does not change what came before, and forgiveness does not fix all of what's been done.

I must understand the story of my mother in order to understand myself, but the truth is I don't know it, not all of it, although I can give pieces. Like how during a visit at my godmother's she decided to pull out all of the old family albums. My godmother is my mother's cousin. Both of their fathers raised them together on neighboring farms. She is one of the few people alive who knew of her then.

My godmother passed over the photos of her own father, my great uncle, turning the fading pages until she found the few of my grandfather. They were photos I'd seen before, most of them taken right before he died.

She turned another page and found the program from his funeral. She read out loud to me the obituary. "Look at that," she said after she'd finished. "There's nothing here. What kind of man has nothing good said about him in his own obituary? What kind of man must he have been?"

"He beat her, she told me that," I said, surprising myself with the sudden declaration. "He was obsessive and controlling. She was afraid of him, and I think he, I think—"

I stopped, not being able to say it. I couldn't bring myself to finish.

My godmother closed the album and placed it on the floor. "I've been thinking about how I'd gone there to help her pack up her things," she said. "It was after we all learned about the cancer, that at this point it was terminal, and I'd gone there to help her decide what would go where and with whom, and we were toward the end of it. The whole thing had been hard, listening to her make all of those decisions, watching her, and then we both got to talking. I don't know how or why but it came up and I just said to her, 'You don't have to tell me, you don't have to say it, but I know something happened. Something happened in that house with you and I'm sorry it's taken me so long to finally put it together, but I know now and I'm sorry.'"

I was quiet then, an echo of my mother's own response. There was nothing for me to say because I did not know how to make peace with knowledge such as this. I was unable to forgive when I was, am, still unsure of the depths of this pain.

Forgiveness is always what is asked of us, but I think of the mothers of men who've been killed. Mothers who've watched the deaths of their sons filmed, their last breaths documented for public consumption for all the world to see, and then having to console themselves with the knowledge that this is necessary—that strangers can see their sons shot in the backs, to see them fall into the grass and dirt, to see them choke and struggle for air, to see them struggle to stay alive—because if others did not see it would not be believed. Even after seeing there are those who do not believe.

I think of the fathers and sisters and brothers and sons of those who'd come to a place of worship and were killed in a massacre of hate. I think of how after, they'd looked into the face of the man who did it, who would maybe even now kill them if he could, and yet still they looked at him and preached forgiveness.

I think of all the ways so many of us live in this world. The injustices we face, the indignities, the shame. The ways in which the measure of ourselves becomes slowly reduced until we no longer recognize ourselves, no longer know the value of who we are. To be black in this world and not be filled with hate means at times having an unlimited amount of grace, because still so many of us continue to forgive.

In an interview, Lezley McSpadden looked toward the camera and explained how she'll never forgive for what's been done to her son, she will never forgive for the taking of his life. As I watched the interview, her statement to me felt like a salve. Her refusal to forgive and let go despite the public's desire for her to do so. I played the recording of it again and observed her frustrations over the injustice. Her anger soothed, and I listened, and my own heart felt saved.

Earlier this summer I was walking out of a movie theater into the sun when I felt the buzz of my phone. It was a friend of mine who I hadn't heard from much since the semester ended. "Finally, I was beginning to worry about you," I say upon answering.

She explains how she'd been busy with packing up her belongings. She graduated a few weeks ago and is now moving across the country. "I'm finally checking my messages and I saw you called. How are you? What are you doing?"

"I was watching a movie. It's over now though."

She asks what I went to see and instead of giving the title I explain the premise. "It centers around the plight of a white Mississippi famer, this man Newton Knight, a deserter of the Civil War who organized a company of men to fight against the Confederates."

"Oh, I saw that," she says. "Or I went to see it but I only got through part of it before I had to leave. It went longer than I was expecting. What happened during the rest of it?"

"The film shifts to Reconstruction. Did you see that part?"

"No, I left right before."

"I was glad the film didn't stop with the end of the war and Reconstruction was also shown even though it was brief. You know, for blacks Reconstruction held this sort of promise and in the film you can see the beginning of that promise—they showed the Freedmen's Bureau meetings and the first black schools being built. It was a moment where there was the belief that the course seemed to be changing, but then the backlash happens."

"Like now," she says. "Post-racial America."

"Yeah," I say, waiting to a few seconds before going on. "Still, there are these huge swaths of in-between time that it seems people forget or don't want to think about when we remember black history. It's always the Civil War, then Jim Crow and lynching, and then the Civil Rights Movement, and like you said I guess now it will be Obama."

"I wish I'd finished the film. I need to go back and see it again. Maybe we can go together before I leave."

"I'd like to," I say. "What's interesting is I knew about Newton Knight but I didn't know about his relationship with Rachel."

Rachel was Newton's grandfather's former slave. Newton took up a common-law marriage with her and together they had five children. However, Newton also previously had nine other children with his white wife, Serena. Newton and Serena separated but never divorced, and they all lived together between two separate houses on Newton's 160-acre plot of land.

The story between the three of them reminds me of my own family's history. "It makes me wonder," I tell my friend. "You know, about what I've been trying to research. I see a film like that and I think maybe it was possible that he claimed them in some way, that he gave at least one of them his name, and that he was more than what I've always believed."

"Or maybe he wasn't," she says, and then I remember Eliza's story. I remember again that the miscegenation laws outlawed black women's marriages to white men, and how the relationships between free black women and white men were defined by law as "fornication." I convince myself that even if their relationship was consensual the outcome would have been the same—he would picked another, married another, had children with another. "You still haven't found out anything either way?"

"No, no record of anything and so I just keep going back and forth, aligning myself one way and then another. Maybe she was raped. Maybe it was consensual. Maybe he left her. Maybe he didn't have a choice. Maybe they all lived together on neighboring plots of land. Maybe he kicked her off. Maybe she sought vindication for what he'd done. Maybe he felt guilt over what he didn't do. I don't know. None of it makes much sense and I am tired of trying to understand."

She listens to me talk for a few minutes more before interrupting. "I don't understand how you're able to think about all of this and not just want to hate all white people," she says. "Because if it was me I would."

It has been a long year for both of us, what with the protests at our university and their repercussions. Her comment relays her own exasperations for the racism present in the town we live in as well as the failures of the people in our program—for the length of time they were silent, and their sudden desire to get to the forefront to speak after the news went national. Like me, she is upset over their ignorance and their hypocrisy, and now their guilt has filled them with ideas of diversity trainings and workshops, with reply-all emails about colloquiums to discuss topical "race relations" texts, but no amount of guilt can save them from themselves.

"I don't know," I say, and even though I can sense her dissatisfaction with my answer, she lets me change the subject.

My mother was not one for forgiveness. When my father left her, when they finally got divorced, she decided that instead of forgiveness she would turn to hate, and through the years she convinced me to hate him too.

Towards the end of her life she would apologize. "I am sorry for what I did," she said. "For making you hate him, but you're going to have to learn how to forgive."

"Why?"

"Because soon he'll be all that you have left."

She paused, and we both thought about the weight of her words. "You're going to have to forgive me too," she said.

*"Your father left us both, you know,"* my mother used to say. *"He didn't want you either."* I've never known the whole story between them but a part of me continues to hold on to her truth. I know one day I will have to ask him for his. I know one day he will tell me and I will have to forgive, but for now I am not ready to go down that path.

"Get your research done?" he asks me upon seeing me walk in the door. I've come back briefly over the summer to visit before driving back home for work. During the past few days I'd gone to the state archives downtown looking through whatever records I could find.

My father believes I am doing researching for a book but he does not know on what and he does not ask. I should tell him, but to do so is to tell him not just about Leanna but to tell him about her children, and I know that the end of that story will lead me back to my mother and what may have happened to her, and why she was the way she was, and I know that eventually it will lead back to us and the reason for this distance we've created.

Instead, I keep my answers vague. "For today," I tell him. "I'm tired though."

"Have you been able to find what you were looking for?"

"Not yet."

My father nods and then focuses his attention elsewhere. I go upstairs and empty my bag on the floor, sit down and look through the copied images of the records I've found.

I should let go of this, I think. I should just forget it and move on, but somewhere in this story is the root of something I need to understand to explain all of what came after.

There is not much about Leanna I've been able to learn, but from what I know of her life it is one that in every way feels fraught with instability and pain.

He could have loved her, I think. He could have loved her but left her still. He was young at the time, far younger than I am now, and the world had taught him to believe she was nothing more than a possession to be used and disregarded.

In every conjured potentiality of this past there is an action needing forgiveness, but the question I have often wondered is if she gave it.

Could you do it? Could I? What if, in the end, it was the only choice you had? Would you still hold on to that hate to pass down to your children? *"She went and had 'em up,"* the story goes. *"She had 'em up,"* is the story passed on. To me that is an action of vindication, of revenge. A punishment for the hurt she endured.

But what if he claimed them in some way, however small? There is no indication to lead to this conclusion beyond folklore, beyond the name carried down, and yet—suppose it happened. Suppose for me a different outcome. Suppose instead, it was enough for her to forgive him for what he'd done. Suppose this one acquiescence was enough. For what he continued to do every day he was alive—for marrying another, for letting the standards of the era dictate his own morality, for his denial of these children.

Suppose for all of this, she forgave anyway, believing it to be her only course to saving herself. Suppose forgiveness could do that. Suppose it was possible. Suppose it was necessary. Suppose that forgiveness, if for a moment, could be what finally set her free.

# Glory Be Her Name

"So I guess we're related," I say light-heartedly to her on the phone.

"Yeah, how about that? I guess we are."

Earlier this afternoon I'd received an email from a woman who'd read one of my essays. *I believe I am someone you're looking for,* her response read, then she explained how the woman I'd written about in the essay, Leanna Brown, was also one of her ancestors.

One night over thirteen years ago I'd decided to browse through a genealogy forum where I'd seen this post—*Seeking information on the mixed or african american siddle family. Possible starting with a Billie Siddle.* I'd replied to the message and hoped for a response but nothing ever came. Nothing, that is, until this email in which she explains how she is the person I'd tried contacting all those years ago.

She'd listed her number at the bottom of the email in case I wanted to get in touch with her. I wrote back almost immediately. *Yes, how about today? What time works best for me to give you a call?*

Now on the phone I listen to her try and map out the link between us. She goes through the line, rapidly listing off each of the names. "Which one of her children do you come down on again?"

"The boy," I tell her. "Willie. He would have been my great, great grandfather I guess."

"Okay, so, let me see," she says, pausing. "That would make us third cousins I think. Yeah, that's right. We're third cousins."

"You did that faster than I ever could have."

She laughs. "Yeah, well, it's not that hard when you've had a little practice."

There is a story I once believed and it begins like this—a woman named Leanna Brown was a slave to Bedford Brown, Senator of North Carolina. Sometime during her enslavement she had a relationship with a white man who lived on a neighboring farm, and the results of their relationship produced three children, one of them my ancestor.

As I hedge closer to the truth, I know some of those pieces are incorrect. Yes, she was a slave, and most likely she was a slave to Bedford Brown, although in looking at his slave population schedules there are none listed fitting her age and description. She had a relationship with someone that produced three children. In looking at the 1870 census, the next one taken after the war, she's living with David Swift and his family, and so perhaps a reasonable assumption would be that maybe he is the father, that maybe he had an affair, and I would consider this possibility except one of those children, the boy, took the surname of a white man by the name of Siddle.

The Siddle family knew the Browns, this I am sure. They bought close to five hundred acres of land from Bedford Brown's estate after he passed away. "Proximity," I've often told my godmother when I lament about my search. "The closest I seem to get is establishing proximity, but nothing beyond that."

"It's a start though," she'd say, her response always managing to prompt me back toward looking.

While I can assume Leanna and Willie had a relationship, it is the particulars of it that I have questioned, just like the particulars of Leanna's life. It is because these are the pieces I've yet to learn that I'm unable to let it go, believing somehow if I go a little further, if I just dig deeper. I look at the name passed down and it is a fact that I can't explain. If they were not married, if she was not his slave, then how did this child come to take his name? How did these children come to exist?

For a while I'd stopped thinking about all of this. After a series of red herrings and false starts, I told myself I needed a break, pushing all of what

I'd found to the side. I have to go to my desk and search a moment to find all of the notes I've collected. There's a corkboard on the floor I'd used to try and map out the genealogy and I lift it up to look at what I'd written.

The woman on the phone tells me she is a descendant of the third child, the youngest, the one Leanna lived with right before she died.

"Lillie," I say, remembering and I imagine her on the other line nodding in response. I look at what I'd written on one notecard—Lillie Bedford, mother Leanna Brown. Father, John Smiley.

"I just have so many questions. Maybe you can help me out with some of them?"

I ask her about Leanna's death, the largest piece of her story that's bothered me, and she says it was a house fire. "She'd been living with her daughter and her husband, and she was getting old so you know. It was very tragic," she tells me. "That's all I know, all that was told to me."

"But she was a fighter," I say, feeling the need to clarify. "She lived for a month with those burns."

"Yes, she did."

She too had tried researching about Leanna and she tells me bits and pieces of what she's learned. While most of it is about the daughter, every now and then she offers another anecdote about the son. "Willie was one of the witnesses to Lillie's wedding," she says. "I always found that nice. That both him and Leanna were there."

"So you saw the actual record?"

"Oh yeah, you know there are always mistakes. It said on one of the census records that her father was a man named Smiley and that's incorrect. You never know. So you have to go and look at the actual thing."

I've found this out the hard way when I searched through census records. *Leanna, Leak, Lena, Leah.* So many variations of the same person. So many errors. So many ways in which a person could easily disappear if one weren't careful in their looking.

I pick up the notecard I'd written with Lillie's name. "So John Smiley is not the father?"

"No, that name is incorrect. That's not her father."

"I know the family always wondered if she was actually Willie's daughter," I say. "The story was that because she was born later, closer toward when Reconstruction was sort of falling apart, that maybe Leanna lost whatever right she had to getting that child the same name as the father. But I've looked at the records and it seems as if neither of the women have his name, only the male child."

"That would make sense when you think about it. It's the male child that carries on the name. Maybe that's how she convinced him to do it. So she would have some link, and the children, back to who they were."

"It's a decision that took an incredible amount of foresight," I say.

She tells me stories about Willie her family told her. Anecdotes I'd never heard before. "He was likeable," she says, interrupting my thought. "He was also very thrifty. When he went to work in the coal mines, he always saved his money. Every penny. You know they would get their allotted rations, their pork or whatever, and one time he accidentally burned his and he ate it anyway. He was careful with what he'd been given."

"Because he saved that money and ended up being able to buy a lot of land that he built on their house on. It was close to three hundred acres."

I stop myself from continuing, thinking of the family he raised, how after he died his wife, now a woman alone with several children in an area surrounded by the Klan, was one day greeted with men who'd asked for her deed. She'd offered it and when it was given back to her the acreage had been altered. Their land lost—stolen.

Like Leanna she did the best she could with the circumstances surrounding her life. Like Leanna she was given a difficult situation, and even though my first instinct is to fault her for letting go of the deed, I've learned that sometimes this world presents itself with a singular choice.

Which is why when I think of Leanna I wonder. She somehow made a different choice. *She had 'em up,* my family used to say. *She took that man to court she he would acknowledge what he'd done.*

"Leanna," I say, shifting the conversation back. "Tell me what you've heard."

It is easy to frame Leanna's life under tragedy. There is an entire history that propels this conclusion to the forefront. While black men could be lynched, castrated, or imprisoned for even the accusation of rape, white men faced no legal ramifications for sexually assaulting black women. Black women were not women according to law, and so they were raped and abused while their stories of victimization largely went unheard.

I know the stories of fancy girls, light-skinned women and girls who were sold off as concubines. I've learned of Thomas Jefferson's sexual assault of fourteen-year-old Sally Hemings, an assault that produced six children. I've read about Harriet Jacobs and the house her master built to rape her in.

Even within these stories there are examples of survival. Harriet Jacobs escaped from her master's sexual advances and hid in her grandmother's attic crawlspace for seven years. Harriet Tubman, our Moses, who followed the North Star toward freedom, who then shepherded hundreds more to escape.

Then there is Celia, a nineteen-year old slave girl who was raped for five years by her master before she finally decided she'd had enough, clubbing him one night when he came to her cabin and burning his body in the fireplace.

It is these stories of survival I hold on to, these moments in which these women reclaimed their agency. They are a reminder to me of the strength of women, the same strength, I hope, that runs through me.

"Ain't I A Woman?" Sojourner Truth asked, and I've wondered it when I've looked at the outline of my lips and I've wondered it when I looked at the stance of my hips and I've wondered it smelling the sulfur taming my hair from the kink.

I've wondered it when I think of my mother's three white dolls, the only ones she had growing up, and I wondered it when she told me once how she preferred to call herself Creole in an avoidance her blackness.

I wondered this question when I think of Leslie Jones. Her private information hacked, nude photos of her body exposed for the world to see. A video of a gorilla who was shot and killed at a Cincinnati zoo prominently posted on the top of her website.

The attack on Jones reminding me of the Washington mayor who ranted about Michelle Obama's "gorilla face." The association not an unfamiliar one in our culture. Scientific racists made claims about how blacks were genetically inferior, closer to primates as a species than Europeans. Around the turn of the 19th century the depiction of the coon caricature became mainstream, especially popular on postcards.

I am reminded of it when I think of the women who've also been victims and yet their stories are often erased from the larger narrative of police violence. Women who've been dragged from their cars, shot inside their homes, killed with their children near.

And I've been reminded of this question during all the years of my life in which I've learned the shame of my skin, of my lips and my hair, and the shame of my thighs. It has existed so long that I do not know when it did not make up a part of who I am, because even as a child I remember sitting in the tub, a washcloth between my hands, as I scrubbed my skin raw, wishing afterward that the water wouldn't be so clear.

"Ain't I A Woman?" I've wondered, but also—*ain't I enough?*

Up until now I have given you one story of my mother but I must tell you of another. In college, she was diagnosed with lupus and the doctors predicted she would not live much farther into adulthood but she did so anyway. She was a woman not meant to have children but she got pregnant with me anyway. Three months before I was meant to be born, she got bit by a brown recluse spider. The combination of the bite and her illness forced her into labor. The doctors did not believe she would survive the delivery but she did anyway.

When I think of my mother, I think of the time a man she was seeing stole her car and went on a joyride through the city. Throughout the night my mother drove in my borrowed car searching, at last finding him in a parking lot smoking with a group of women where in a wild fury she managed to grab him and drag him out of the car.

I think of the time she came home, having picked up a stranger she found standing outside of the Walmart looking for work. She'd offered him a deal, cut our grass and she'd cook him dinner and give him a little cash and he'd agreed. I watched my mother stand in our kitchen as she sliced pieces of leftover meatloaf to put in a container.

"Are you crazy?" I asked her. "Why would you bring him home? You don't know who he is."

"He's fine," she said calmly. "Besides, he needs help."

Alone, with an illness, with mounting debt, and working several jobs that never paid enough, still my mother managed to raise me. It took the man she loved leaving to break her, and then loving another man who would not leave his wife to break her again.

She would get pregnant and decide not to keep it. "It is the one thing I regret," she told me, "but what was I supposed to do? I made a choice and now I have to live with it."

The last job my mother had before she died was working the night shift in a correctional facility for inmates with mental illness. "I feel bad for some of them. I wish there was more I could do," she'd say, refusing to tell me more beyond that. Sometimes she had nightmares and I would hear her crying out in her sleep.

When I think of my mother, I think of how after she got sick she kept it a secret from me until the very end, until it became impossible to hide it from me any longer. She was afraid it would keep me from graduating college. She did not want me to follow the same pattern of her life. She hid it so I could finish, and even though it almost broke me to do it, I finished.

My mother was a woman who did not know the full potentiality of her power, who died unknowing the possibilities of her life.

"I have one last question," I say on the phone, pausing. "Do you know anything about the photo?"

I tell her about the picture I found. A copy of a framed portrait taken of Leanna, the only image I've ever seen of her.

"Oh yes, I have the original. I'm the one that put it out there. I think I'd even passed a copy along to the county historical association," she explains.

"I was wondering where it came from. What kind of image is it? I couldn't tell."

"It's an old tintype. They were pretty common for the era I think. It was painted over because the image was starting to fade so that's why it looks like that."

"What about her in the photo? She looks—I mean, I don't know. I don't know all that much about this period, but to me she looks—"

"Taken care of," she says, interrupting. "She looks well taken care of and well loved."

I wait a moment to see if she'll go further, if she'll offer the suggestion that has been on my mind, but when she's quiet I decide to bring it up anyway. "I've often wondered if maybe, and I'm hypothesizing here, I can't prove this at all, but I've wondered if the reason for that, I mean she's so light, and she looks so young in the photo, so I thought maybe it's because she's possibly related to him or the family in some way."

"I'd never considered that."

"Because why her?" I say, my voice picking up. "The man had a lot of slaves. Why is she the one that worked in the house? Why was she one that looks so taken care of?"

"I mean, it could be. It's possible. It might explain why I couldn't find her in his slave census records."

"I don't know the answer. It's just something I've thought about. Another piece I can't prove. Gosh, I just don't know. I don't know about any of it. Her life then or even after the war. None of it makes sense."

"You know, what I've found interesting is that she's listed as keeping house in that 1880 census you mentioned. Keeping house meant you were a woman at home, tending to the house, and she's a woman listed living at home with three children."

"Right, so the question is who's taking care of those children."

"And who's taking care of her?"

"And why?"

"Exactly."

"Another piece I've thought about—the children all came after slavery, but the second one, I guess your great-grandmother, if you look at the timeline and trace it back, she was conceived right around the time he gets married."

"I didn't know that."

"So, that story, the 'had 'em up' story, I've wondered if there was a connection there, like her taking him to task, so to speak, but you know I just have so many theories about all of this."

"I mean, it's possible."

"I guess I'm interested in that idea because it brings forth another way of looking at the story. It's another way of examining her life."

"It is true that there were women who took the white fathers to court," she says, echoing my godmother's response.

"But then I think of that area during that time frame and it just seems."

"Yeah, it seems crazy," she says. "Her whole life. She's always been someone who's fascinated me. Her life was just—"

"I know," I say.

"I think she would be happy you are telling this story. That someone hadn't forgotten about her."

"I'd like to see that deed. You said all their names are on it?"

"Yeah, it's the only thing I've found that has all their names on it, that connects them all together in any kind of way, and it mentions how all their land bordered each other. I can't believe after all this time it's all I got, and I almost even missed it altogether, but it is what it is."

I tell her I'll send a copy of the deed and she'll try and get together copies of whatever records she's found. "I think I may have pictures too," she says.

I'm about to hang up when I remember one last question. "Have you ever contacted any of the white side? Heard from any of them? I'm curious to know what story they know about it, what they were told, if anything."

"No, I never got in touch with any of them."

"I wonder what they know. I've thought about trying, but I'm not sure if anyone would still be alive to even know anything about it."

"For what it's worth, I think you're close. Somewhere in those records is the answer you're looking for. You might try the apprentice bonds, if you ever get a chance to go. They're often neglected records when people are searching. If you can find one her name would be listed as the parent, and his too possibly, either as the father but if he was apprenticeship master—it would give further credence."

"I wouldn't have even thought to look at those."

"It's another possibility," she says. "Like I said, there's something somewhere. I would bet money. It's really just a matter of finding it."

Chimamanda Ngozi Adichie spoke about the danger of a single story, but what of the danger of no story? What if when you look for representations of you, you find nothing there?

Once, in a class, we were discussing a student's piece. It was the first few chapters of a novel where the protagonist was a young black girl attending a mostly white school. It was a story about the ways in which one's environment can contribute to feelings of self-hate.

It was a familiar story, with echoes of moments I'd read about before. We were talking about a scene where the protagonist recognizes her difference, a moment recalling Frantz Fanon's, a moment that every one of us experiences—when we recognize not only our difference but that the world sees us as inferior.

A couple of classes before we'd read Toni Morrison's "Recitatif," a story about race that removes all racial codes. The timing of both of these together had been unexpected but appropriate.

"I never—I never really thought about any of these before. I guess I never had reason to," one of my students says in a low voice.

Because I knew if I pushed too hard I would lose them, I decided not to talk about the lack of diversity in publishing. Instead, I tried a different approach. I asked them a simple question. "When you're writing, when you're reading, if no race is mentioned, what are you picturing? Is it always a white person?"

They were quiet as they thought about my question. My students didn't answer because we all knew the answer. White was the default. White was the story, and so it'd become ingrained in them to picture one answer and it was only now, perhaps in this moment, when they'd finally begun to question the reason why.

"I think about this a lot, how when I construct my own stories, often the image in my own head is white. That's a problem, but I'm not sure how to fix it," I say, continuing. "Even in my own mind I have erased myself."

I never sent her the deed. A few weeks after the phone call, I remembered I was supposed to mail a copy. I went through my files and looked at the document again. I read over the names—William Siddle, Laura Siddle, and L. Brown.

"Oh, damn."

It did not occur to me then who else the "L. Brown" could be but now it was obvious. Livingston Brown. Bedford Brown's son and executor of his estate. It was not Leanna at all.

I thought I had something. It felt like a secret when I found it tucked away amongst so many other miscellaneous records. I believed it had been waiting there for me throughout all these years. I'd held that document in my hands and it seemed like, for a moment, I had finally found a piece of her and her story.

What bothers me is not that I was wrong. In thinking of Leanna, I am reminded of how so many of our stories are determined by who is able to give voice to them. I think often of this unheard chorus of women. Who they were, their dreams and desires, pains and heartaches, the intricacies of their lives—it is all lost to us. They have all but disappeared.

"There is power in looking," bell hooks writes, and glory be the name of those who showed me the way, who showed me that there was another way of seeing, and I see now Marley Dias who took it upon herself to solve the lack of representation in the books at her school. I see Misty Copeland, the first African American woman named principal dancer of the American Ballet Theatre, but also of Raven Wilkinson and Janet Collins and Lauren Anderson and Carmen Lavallade.

I am interested in a different story now. Tell me not a story of broken-ness but of the ways we have fought and survived. Yes, tell me of the men who fought in the war for our freedom, but tell of the women too. Tell me of Mary Bowser, known to have a photographic memory, who assumed the identity of an illiterate slave in the Confederate White House. She snuck out information to Union forces about troop movements, Union prisoner locations, and military strategies. Tell me of Mary Touvestre, housekeeper of the Confederate engineers, who stole a set of plans for the building of the CSS Virginia and traveled to Washington, managing to meet with the Secretary of the Navy.

Countee spoke of a brown girl dead, but show me instead these double-dutch girls playing across my street. The rope crackles against the pavement as they shift their feet to the rhythm. Show me these students on my campus quad dancing to "Formation" while their white peers look on. Show me the women who have let down the wild glory of their hair, proclaiming beauty in all its variations while being unafraid and unashamed. Give me the stories from those whose love of their blackness came from a love of themselves. Tell me of the history of women we have overlooked—those who marched alongside you in Washington, who stood behind as you traveled to that mountaintop. Tell me these stories of the women forgotten, women lost, women with their own dreams deferred. Tell me of the darker sisters who cooked your meals in the kitchen, who made heaven from scraps to fuel your children so they also could grow strong. Where now is their seat at this table, so beautifully prepared? They, too, have sung America, have built this America, and it is time to tell their stories of how.

This is my call.

*I write for women like us,* someone told me once, a friend, and I am reminded of this every time I look on the screen and see a woman who looks like me or when I hold a book in my hands from someone who looks like me or when I see a woman who looks like me on the street unconcerned with the stares of the world. Each time I am reminded me that there is more than one way of being.

Once, she came to visit and we were sitting in a bar having a drink. The night was winding down, last calls were being asked for.

"I just want to say," I began, stumbling through the words. I looked at my watered-down drink, held the glass between my hands, and I realized I couldn't finish what it was I wanted to say.

I am not sure what I eventually said to her after I had broken the silence, but if I had the moment to do over, if we could have gone back to the beginning, I would have said this—I did not know who I was until I saw you, and I did not know all of what I could be.

And so, I think of others who are still waiting to get to the place I've finally come to, and I think of the women with stories of their lives we've yet to hear. I know you are out there. I know you are waiting, and to you I say, someone is listening. Someone is waiting to hear, so tell me. So come forth, and let's begin.

# The Inheritors

In the center of the Yanceyville town square is a monument of a Confederate soldier. It is the first thing I notice when I pull up here. I've seen images of it before when I looked at photos of the courthouse. The soldier stands tall, proud even, looking northward as he grasps his rifle. He is on a pedestal, high above the rest. Inhabitants of the town literally look up to him as they drive around the square. The United Daughters of the Confederacy erected the monument in 1921. During their unveiling ceremony the audience sang "America" as well as the "Dixie" song. Below the statue is this inscription—*to the sons of Caswell County who served in the War of 1861-1865 in answer to the call of their country, in whatever event that may face our national existence may God give us the will to do what is right, that like our forefathers, we may impress our time with the sincerity and steadfastness of our lives.*

Across the country others are fighting to remove memorials such as this, memorials that the United Daughters of the Confederacy worked to litter the South with. Memorials like in Birmingham and Louisville and Dallas. In New Orleans, plans to remove the imposing monuments of Robert E. Lee and P.G.T. Beauregard were met with death threats and the torching of one contractor's car. A few months ago in the town where I live, there was a petition to move the 11,000-pound memorial known as "Confederate Rock" off the county courthouse property.

"I don't mind the statues, as long as they're there and open for everyone, then they can have their memorials of history, but I want ours too. Where are ours?" My godmother's words are on my mind as I stare up at this memorial.

It has taken me a couple of hours to get to this place. Caswell County is situated right on the border between North Carolina and Virginia. Its proximity to Virginia has made research about my ancestors difficult. That and Caswell County is made up mostly of a number of small unincorporated communities. There's Casville and Prospect Hill, Pelham and Quick. *"You never wanted to stay long in Quick,"* my mother used to say, *"and you never wanted to be near it once it got dark."* Near Quick is Ruffin, the area where my mother grew up. I will go there next but I wanted to come to Yanceyville, the town existing right in the county's center. I came to Yanceyville first mostly because it is large enough to be a town and I knew it could be a place to stop. There are a few mom-and-pop restaurants scattered around and there's the downtown, if one could call it that, which consists of this town square.

I stand in front of the statue but look beyond it, because there is the courthouse, the only antebellum public building left in the county. In the basement of this courthouse a senator was assassinated by members of the Ku Klux Klan. John "Chicken" Stephens, Republican state senator, who'd been an agent of the Freedmen's Bureau and an active member of the Union League. I learned about Chicken Stephens through trying to find more information about Bedford Brown. Stephens was elected as the state senator over Brown, and in researching this I learned about the murder. The Klan had gathered earlier to decide Stephens' fate, held a "trial" *in absentia* of Stephens where they sentenced him to death. Former Democratic sheriff Frank Wiley lured Stephens down the stairs of the courthouse where other Klansmen were waiting, and the moment Stephens finished coming down the steps they were on him. They stabbed him to death and left his body to bleed out on a woodpile while they all went back upstairs to finish with the meetings being held in the courthouse.

A few months earlier in a nearby county another man was lynched. Wyatt Outlaw, the first African American Town Commissioner and Constable of Graham, was hung from a tree in the courthouse square. On his chest was the message, "Beware, ye guilty, both black and white."

These two events sparked an insurrection known as the Kirk-Holden War. Governor William Holden imposed martial law on Caswell and Alamance counties and sent in troops. Around a hundred men were arrested, some highly respected members of the community. Holden had instructed that the writ of habeas corpus be suspended. Lawyers sent out requests to the Chief Justice of the Supreme Court, which were granted but then ignored at the instruction of Governor Holden. They were taken to federal court where a federal judge ordered all but a few released, and those that weren't were never tried. The fallout from this insurrection led to the impeachment of Governor Holden. He was impeached, convicted, and removed from office for his perceived wrongdoing.

When all of this was close to over, the former senator Bedford Brown would pass away in his home. His son Livingston became the executor of his estate, and three tracts of his land, totaling over 300 acres, were sold to a white family by the name of Siddle. A father and his two sons. One of them built a general and liquor store and became relatively successful with his business. The other son farmed the land. He soon met a girl, perhaps already had met her. A girl who was once a slave but now was not, who like him also worked the land, or on it, and just before this man decided to marry another, she would have two, maybe three, of his children. One of those children will take on his surname.

To me it seems an impossible thing to have happened, to believe that they could have had a relationship, even taking into account that he eventually would marry someone else. Not far from here, in Eden, one of the largest groups of the KKK is located. Just a few years ago in Reidsville, a town my grandmother lived in before she died, the Loyal White Knights of the KKK invited residents to a "whites only" cross burning. So to imagine a situation in which this man could have acknowledged, claimed, any of these children is difficult.

I stare out at this two-story masonry structure with its domed cupola. I should go inside, at least see the courtroom with its original 19th-century decorations, and I will go, but before I do I take out my phone to finally call my godmother.

"You made it!" she exclaims upon the first ring.

"Yeah, I'm here. I'm in Yanceyville."

"So what are you going to do first? Are you going to go through the records that are there?"

"No, I—" I pause, looking around the square. The library is in one direction and in another is the newer courthouse where the more current records are kept. A block away is the Richmond-Miles Museum containing county artifacts. There is not much time to do everything, even waiting here I know I am wasting it and need to make a decision. "What about the house?" I finally ask her. "Tell me how to get to the house."

North Carolina, once hailed the "Tobacco State," is tobacco country. Among its counties Caswell used to be one to the richest in the state with tobacco being its leading agricultural product. In 1860 there were only two other counties that exceeded the amount of pounds of tobacco produced. In Caswell it was tobacco, not cotton, that was king. One of the reasons for this is due to the invention of Bright Leaf, or flue-cured tobacco. Flue-cured tobacco could grow in even the poorest soil, providing opportunity to struggling farms.

Flue-cured tobacco was born here. The story told is that of Abisha Slade's slave Stephen. During the night Stephen fell asleep while watching the wood fires in the barn used for curing the tobacco. By coincidence he'd awoken to salvage the dying fire. He threw charred log butts in, and the combination of the dry heat from the charred logs caused the leaves to turn a bright yellow color. Abisha decided to sell Stephen's mistake anyway, calling it Bright Leaf tobacco, and it quickly grew in popularity, becoming the state's signature.

"That story!" my godmother exclaimed when I reminded her of it. She doesn't have to explain because I know what she's going to say—the familiar stereotype so embedded in our culture. "I've never fully believed it. Never believed it happened the way it did."

Tobacco is rooted not just in North Carolina's history but in our country's. It was the first crop planted in Jamestown. It was tobacco that George Washington issued to his troops during the Revolutionary War.

Tobacco leaves are embedded architecturally in the structure of capital buildings, including being incorporated in the U.S. Capitol's Hall of Columns. During the Civil War, tobacco revenues help fund the war effort in the North and a tobacco tax helped in the South. In WWII, General John Pershing believed that tobacco helped men cope with the stress of battle and so he urged the government to send it to the soldiers, including it in the soldiers' rations.

Tobacco is a thirteen-month crop. The process of flue-curing began in early January when farmers would prepare the seed beds for planting. By the next month they would plant the seedbeds and six weeks later the seedlings matured. During that time farmers worked on the main fields, preparing for transplanting. Using a mule they'd plow through the field, breaking up the soil, fertilizing it, making furrows in the dirt. In April the transplanting of the seedbeds into the fields began, and then somewhere around the start of August it would be time to harvest. Farmers would pick the leaves and haul them out of the fields to the barn. There, these leaves were tied and hung on laths in the barn to cure.

When I think of tobacco, I don't think of my mother climbing the rafters of the barn to hang the laths, or the hours of her life she spent underneath the sun toiling with the rest of the family to pick the leaves, nor of any of my ancestors who built their livelihoods from the plant. No, when I think of tobacco I think of how in the old way, each year the soil was burned. It seems counter-intuitive, to destroy in the hopes to grow, but the burn had several objectives. It removed competition from weeds. It prepared the ground for the next cycle of crops, and in this way the soil could be made anew.

My godmother thinks I mean my mother's house, but that is not what I mean. I meant Bedford Brown's house, known as Rose Hill, and I meant the road. I've been told that this road was once known colloquially as Siddle Road and it connected two properties—on one end Senator Bedford Brown's land and on the other a family of white farmers. It is the idea of this road that has made me ponder the possibilities. This road, this bridge, between a once slave and a white farmer. After all these years it is what has finally brought me back.

So I am not prepared when instead she gives me the directions to my mother's childhood house, and I am not prepared when she tells me the man who owns the property will come and let me on the land, and I am not prepared for when I drive down the road and I see it.

I was a child when I last came here, and when I think of it I think of my family packing up boxes. I think of the house as mostly empty and dark, because it was evening when we came, the sun having long gone. I have dreamt of this place many times in the years since and it is always full of darkness, of shadows, and an overwhelming sense of urgency to leave it.

The house now is falling into disrepair. It needs new paint, and from my view it seems to be filled with junk. The man I've come to meet says as much. His name is Eddie and he is soft-spoken with a kind face. "I'm working on fixing it all up. If I'd known a little earlier I'd have tried to at least clean it out," he says, almost mournfully. "Right now there—there's a lot of stuff inside. It's not really a good idea anyway to be going around up in there."

Even if the offer was available I'm not sure I would. It is almost too much to think of what happened here, and I am glad I'm unable to go inside. Instead, I tell him I just want to take a few pictures, if it's all right, and he nods.

As I look at the house I try to remember the stories of its layout. *Your uncle and I shared a room on the first floor, and in order to get out I had to go through my parent's bedroom. I remember creeping across the wood floor and praying neither would wake. Upstairs Pigaboy lived. He wasn't allowed downstairs, came down the steps through this foyer toward the back of the house where he got his meals.*

I follow the perimeter, pausing only once to try and see inside one of the windows. To the left of me are woods. I walk toward them but I can't see much beyond the brush so I go farther, edging as close to it as I can without going in.

"Down that way is the settlement of your great-grandmother's," Eddie says, having followed me a little ways. "It's kind of cool to see something of the 1800s."

He is pitching me to come back, back when more of the woods have been cleared, when the house has been repaired and the junk inside cleaned, when it has become something more than what it is now.

"You want to see the lake?" he asks after I've circled the property and taken my photos.

Eddie's managed to build a lake on the land. He says sometimes he'll bring a boat down there to fish. He wants to take me to see it and explains that even though the path down hasn't been cleared it'll only take him a few minutes to do it.

I tell him he doesn't have to show me, that just being able to see the property is enough, but he persists enough for me to realize that I should go. I get the sense that he's been waiting a long time to show someone all he's done, and so I say okay, getting in my car and following him on his tractor down the path.

After slave labor was lost due to the end of the Civil War, Caswell, like the majority of the south, turned to the sharecropping system. Under sharecropping, families would rent out plots of land to work for themselves. In return at the end of the year they'd give a portion of their crop's yield to the landowner as payment.

Instead of blacks getting their promise of "40 acres and a mule" they instead found themselves in a situation where they were forced to sign labor contracts with white-owned farmers and planters, many of them their former owners, in order to make a living.

In a book about Caswell's history, William S. Powell notes a sharecropping contract made between Bedford Brown and a group of men who'd agreed to work for him. Powell briefly details the contract before explaining how the end of the document had been signed with a mark by several men, with one of them, David Swift, having written his name for himself.

"David Swift," I'd said at the time, repeating the name in the hopes of jogging my memory. It took me a few moments before remembering the 1870 census record I'd copied. Leanna Brown is there listed as a house servant living with David Swift and his family. Her name is misspelled, and she's on the very bottom of the record so in passing it's easy to miss it, but she's there.

"They were probably kindred in some way," my godmother explained when I told her this.

"Related, you mean? Like a brother?"

"Maybe, but not necessarily, but close. To take someone in your home in that way, to take care of them, it implies a kindred type of relationship, especially when you think about the time period."

So Leanna is living with a black family and working for another. *Leanna Brown, house servant.* In the 1880 census she will continue to hold the same position. *Leanna Brown, house servant.* The question then becomes, to who was she a house servant for?

"She could have been a kept woman," my godmother supposed to me once. "She could have worked for the Brown family and then worked for the Siddles. She could have taken care of his kids and he could have helped with money to take care of her own."

"Maybe," I say, but the truth is I don't know the circumstances of their relationship—not how they met, whether their relationship was consensual or if he raped her for years. I do not know if he cared for her. I do not know if she worked for his family. I do not know if his wife knew or his children ever knew. I do not know if he had any part in the land my ancestors inherited, the land my mother's house was built on, the land they all eventually lost.

I follow Eddie for quite a ways down a windy grass hill. The farther we go the more I tense up. We drive until I can go no farther and I stop my car.

"We're going to have to walk now a little."

I'm hesitant at first, but I let him lead me along through a narrow path he's cleared. Along the way he reminds me to be careful of snakes. I try not to think of it as we walk, the sun already blinding and so my hands shield my face. We walk, both of us quiet, and then I see it.

The lake is impressive when you imagine how it was the work of one man. He explains how when he bought the land it was all trees and he had to clear it all away.

"I'm going to build a road so that you can drive on out to the other side and to the highway."

"The property goes that far?"

"Oh yeah. You see all around here," he waves his hand and points off in the distance. "Everything up to the tallest trees is the property line. Your family once owned a lot of land."

*"It felt expansive to us as kids. It was like our own world."* My mother used to tell me, and in the recognition of this a sadness comes over me realizing all that was lost. To put a face to it, to see its breadth and scope, and I have to look away.

"I'm just trying to, you know, bring the place to what it used to be. As best as I can get it and for as long as I'm able, God willing, I'm going to try."

My great-grandmother had meant for the land to be a place the family could always come to, but she never made any legal arrangements beyond the verbal expression of her wish. After she died, my grandfather, his brother, and both of their families maintained the farms while the others left—the eldest ones settling up north as part of the Great Migration. After my grandfather died, the family fought like lions over who would inherit the land. At the time, my grandmother was living on the property with her young son, and the family was faced with the decision of what to do with her, if she should be allowed to stay in the house on land that was legally not hers.

"I remember your mother talking about her being in a room with everyone arguing over it. She'd had a tape recorder hidden on her lap. She'd pretended to be knitting but was actually recording the conversation. She couldn't believe how they were, how much they fought."

My grandmother eventually decided to leave on her own and the land got put up for auction and Eddie was the one to put in a bid.

This man has lived here his entire life. He loves this land, seems to love it more than I or anyone else in my family possibly could. As I look at him, I wonder if in the end this is how it should be, and maybe me coming here is kind of letting go.

"You should come back next year," Eddie says after a while. "Come around again and let me know early on. I'll have time to bushwhack all the grass and you'll see, and I'll fix up the house."

"I know some of the family has been wanting to see all this."

"I'd like to show them, show you all what it could be, because it's really something. It really is."

In 2004 North Carolina introduced the Tobacco Transition Payment Program, or the Tobacco Buyout. Farmers faced with disappearing contracts were able to receive compensation for their lost income. The funds for the buyout were initiated from the "Master Settlement Agreement" with the major tobacco companies in 1998. They pledged an estimated $9.6 billion to pay to growers and quota owners "in equal annual installments over ten years."

With the tobacco buyout, the federal government removed all regulation on the quantity and price of tobacco produced. In the past, quotas and pricing regulations determined how much a farmer could grow or what they could expect to earn, but now it was the tobacco companies, the cigarette manufacturers and leaf merchants who could dictate how much is grown through their contracts. They had the power to drive the profit margins per acre of tobacco down, and for those farmers wanting to survive they had to either consolidate or decide to get out of the business altogether.

Tobacco growers consolidated in order to grow more and sustain their farms. They hired contractors to procure field labor, often consisting of undocumented workers and even children.

One does not have to look far to see the patterns. Slavery was a system and with its destruction has come new systems. The sharecropping system. Awhile back I'd made a visit down to Vacherie, Louisiana, had gone to bear witness to the string of plantations along River Road. At the Whitney, my tour guide had finished the tour by making the connection to sharecropping. "It was just another form of slavery," he'd said.

The Black Codes created another system where things like "loitering" and "breaking curfew" became criminal acts, the results of which warranted imprisonment. As convicts men could be leased out to white plantation owners to work their land for free. Then came the rise of chain gangs. Shackled together as they worked, often worked at gunpoint, often under whips. There's the "school-to-prison pipeline" that targets students of color. Children, punished for "zero-tolerance" policies that criminalize minor infractions of school rules, are taken out of the public school system and sent into juvenile and criminal justice systems. The "tough on crime" and "war on drugs" arrests and subsequent convictions, also meant to target men and women of color, for non-violent felonies. The rise in human trafficking of women of color for commercial sexual exploitation or forced labor. The continuing exploitation of prison labor. In Louisiana near the northeast border is the Louisiana State Penitentiary, or Angola Prison. Angola, once a former plantation, is now a maximum security prison farm that was named after the homeland of the slaves that worked on the land.

At the time, I'd wanted my tour guide to go further, to make these connections, but I understood why he didn't. It is a perhaps a hard sell to make people think about the ways this still continues. It is easier to shame the past. It is easier to look back and find our morality.

My father's never been interested in the past, at least not ours. Films about African American history, about slavery or the Civil Rights Movement, he'll pass over despite their popularity. "I don't need to see it when I lived through it," he explained once when I told him about *Selma*.

"What about to remember history?"

"I remember it," he responded.

So it was a surprise when the night before I left my father agreed to the suggestion of *Roots* as the evening entertainment. I imagined it was because I would be gone once morning came, making the long journey back to the town where I live.

The *Roots* miniseries has been remade in hope of engaging a new generation with this connection to the past. Every night they've premiered a new episode of the series, and tonight was the third.

My father appeared agitated as we watched it. He periodically got up and walked to the kitchen, first for a glass of water and then again for a snack. "I can't decide what I want," he said out loud.

"Just pick something," I called back.

He asked me if I'd seen his phone. He sifts through the mail on the counter. "You look through any of these coupons? There might be something here you want."

"Yes, dad, come on, and sit back down."

He opened one of the cabinets, settled on a cup of a coffee. I listened as the water heated up in the machine and finally, realizing my father would not stop until I changed my mind, reached for the remote and paused the show.

"What are you doing? Why'd you stop it?"

"I thought I'd wait for you."

"You, that's all right. You can keep going."

"I'll wait."

He finished with the coffee and settled into the seat on the sofa. "Okay, okay," he said, before taking a long sip from the mug. "Go ahead and hit play now. I'm ready."

My father relied on his memory of the original to orient him, but still asked questions, mainly to keep himself engaged. By the time a commercial came he'd fallen asleep, and I had to wake him back up after the break was over.

"So you're off tomorrow," he said, opening his eyes again. It came out as a statement, a reminder to himself that I was once again leaving. This has been our story for as long as I can remember. It is one of distance and loss, of leaving and goodbyes. He left my mother and he left me, and because of this I have left him ever since.

"Yeah, I'm going to drive back to Caswell County first though. To mom's house."

He seemed surprised by this, as if he'd forgotten I told him this was what I was doing. "Maybe I should come with you? It's been years, decades even, since I've seen that house. I'm curious as to what it looks like now."

"I don't think that's a good idea."

"What not?"

"There's some other stuff I have to do. I need to go it alone, I think."

"Yeah, yeah I figured." He looked up at the screen. "Your mother had a lot of problems."

"I know."

He looked over at me, waiting for me to go further. We've hedged around this conversation a hundred times over the years, each of us hypothesizing, getting closer to what the truth of her life was, while neither of us fully wanting to admit what happened. He refused to be the one to say it first, wanting instead for me to relieve him of the burden, but instead I kept quiet.

"I loved her though," he said quietly. "I don't think I can watch this," he finally admitted before standing up. "I'm sorry, I might watch it another day but I can't right now."

"It's okay."

He explained how he had work to do in his office. Contracts to finish. Since it was late, he went ahead and told me goodnight. "I guess I'll just check you out in the morning," he said before leaving.

I remained in the living room. I turned the volume down low so as not to disturb my father in the other room. For a brief while longer I tried to focus, but my attention was elsewhere. We can love people and they can still be damaged, I thought. We can love them and that love could be everything and yet still not be enough. Before this story ends I must tell you that I loved my mother. I loved her, too.

In the episode of *Roots* we tried to watch, it follows the story of Kizzy, Kunta Kinte's daughter. Kizzy gets auctioned off to a poor farmer by the name of Tom Lea who, upon her first night there, rapes her after she declines his sexual advances. Kizzy becomes pregnant with his son who will be known as Chicken George for his skill training his master's birds for cockfighting. There's a scene in the film where Chicken George and his father have traveled for one such fight and Lea bets on Chicken George's freedom. Right before the fight begins, they announce each of the opponents. "Tom Lea of Caswell County," a man's voice booms in the film.

I've said goodbye to Eddie and am sitting in my car deciding on where to go when I check my phone and see my father's called, most likely to check in and see if I'm okay. Because I don't know where to go next, I call him back in an attempt to stall my decision.

"Just wanted to make sure you were doing okay," he says after he hears my voice.

"Yeah, I'm fine. I saw the house. It wasn't what I expected."

He doesn't ask me to clarify what I mean, instead wonders when I'm heading out.

"Soon," I say.

He tells me that he decided to watch the miniseries. He's been watching it for most the day, actually, starting from the beginning and had now finished the episode we'd started to watch together before he decided he'd had enough.

"In the film they talk about Tom Lea."

"Yeah, the farmer. The father of Chicken George."

"Did you know they mention Caswell? Tom Lea of Caswell County?"

I had not picked up on it the first time and so he describes the scene and then I remember. "Yeah, I guess it was Caswell."

"Tom Lea of Caswell County," he repeats. "Isn't that something? Hey, your grandmother. Wasn't her last name Lea?"

"Yeah, it is. Lea. I'm pretty sure it is."

"That's a pretty small coincidence, don't you think?"

"I hadn't thought about it."

"There's got to be some connection," he says. "You should look into that while you're there."

"I mean, maybe. I don't know."

I don't tell my father that Lea is a popular surname in the county. The idea of researching it would be like finding a needle in a haystack, and there is only so much time. My father though is convinced it is a thread worth pursuing. What are the odds? He tells me. Her family could have been his slaves, he says, and I tell him yes, maybe, probably so.

Once there was a black woman who had a relationship with a white man. They had two, maybe three children, and one of them took his name. The question to how this was possible, and why she did it, is one I'd sought to answer.

"You might never know the story, and you're going to have to be okay with that," my godmother used to tell me. It was always there in the undertone of her responses, it was her way of saying maybe I should let this go.

I did not understand her response then, but I thought of it as I stood in an unlocked room of the public library. I'd decided before I left I'd at least come here, thinking I'd just see what I could possibly find.

The woman at the desk brought me to this room. "We keep a lot of the sort of stuff you're looking for here." She goes to one of the shelves and pulls a couple history books about the county and places them on the table. "This should get you started," she says, then leaves me among the collection.

I glance at the books before turning my attention toward the shelf where they came from. I look at the empty space and then shift my gaze toward what's left, and right there, as if it was waiting for me, is a book of the Caswell County Bible records.

Often located between the Old and New Testaments, these Family Bibles contained "Records" or a "Register" section where the names of births, marriages, and deaths were written among the pages. The front of the Bible could also include family relationships.

The book is a typed account from all the Bible records they found. Because it is not the actual thing I wonder what, if anything, could be left out. Still, I take the book off the shelf and hold it in my hands. If I were to turn and look, to see his name among these pages, to see what he left behind, I know that the answer would not be enough. I know that even if the children were there, were at least named there, it would still not be enough. Like with everything, it will lead me to more questions, more possibilities to the way things were. In the end, what would it change? I will never fully know the story between them, not all of it, like I will never know the story of my mother.

I wonder what our descendants will say about us a hundred years from now, when we are all buried in the family plots of our ancestors or are dust dissolved in the sea, when we are long gone from being able to answer for our actions. Will there be the same questions? *Was it possible there was love? Was it possible they were good? Was the world all filled with hate?*

I wonder what they will say about the people we once were.

After the library I get in my car, realizing there is one more place left for me to go.

"We went down the road a long time ago," I remember my godmother telling me. "We all went there as a family because I wanted the rest of them to see it, at least once in their life to see it, and we drove down a little ways and—I don't know, maybe it was because it was close to dusk and this orange glow had settled over the land, or maybe it was because I knew the place's history and I had all that on my mind, but we started down it and I said we had to turn around. I couldn't do it. An uneasiness settled over me and I didn't want to go farther, didn't want to see anymore, so we turned around and headed back home."

I drive west from Yanceyville on Highway 158. I've entered this address in my navigation system and listen as the voice guides me there.

"You've arrived at your destination," the voice says as I pass by the familiar placard.

"What? That can't be right."

Behind the placard is nothing but dense trees. There's a narrow gravel driveway but from my view I can't see where it leads. On the other side is another road, the way more clear, but I'm not sure if it's the right way either.

I try the one by the placard first. It takes me several attempts of driving back and forth along the highway before I'm able to make the turn. I pull in and ease off the brakes, inching forward, but the closer I move along the closer the brush seems to get to my car, the road begins to narrow further, and it is when I can feel my car slowly start to decline down a hill that I finally stop.

I'm tempted to get out my car and walk it. If I had to guess I'd suspect that somewhere down this road is Bedford Brown's home. Just a little farther past these trees, beyond what I can't see.

I call my godmother again. "Do you remember where it was? Like how far from the placard?"

"It should be right there. Right off it."

"Were there a lot of trees? Because I'm down here and I'm sort of stuck and I'm not sure if this is right. There's this other road but it's not dirt there's gravel."

"That's probably it, but I can't tell you exactly. I mean, it was long ago. I'd have to be there and see it to be sure."

"Okay."

I edge my car back out, slowly making my way to the highway. When it's clear I back out and then make a quick left turn down the gravel road opposite me, and then I stop.

I am not sure if this is it either. To my right is a small brick house that sits close to the highway, but in front of me on both sides of this road is mostly land.

Taking a breath, I press lightly on the gas, going slow so as to limit the amount of dust that clouds the air caused from my tires against the gravel. After a few moments I see two abandoned structures—what look to once be a barn and a tobacco shed. Both are rusted and falling apart. A cluster of round hay bales is in front of them, blocking the entrance. I drive a little farther before I stop my car and get out. I walk to the edge of the field, thinking maybe I'll venture toward the barn, but the thought of rattlesnakes makes me step back on the gravel.

I try to picture it, what it could have looked like then. The rows of tobacco leaves in full bloom. Their homes far off in the background. My ancestors worked this land. This land lost but now found again. They farmed it and they died on it. I know that this will be the closest I'll ever get to a piece of them and an understanding of the life they lived. It is not mine, will never be mine, but I am here. I made it and I am here.

The sun begins its slow descent into the horizon. The heat settles down. It will be dark soon and I should leave before it comes.

"I thought this would feel different," I say out loud.

And yet, I continue waiting, despite knowing there are no answers here, just dirt and grass. Heat. Miles of what appear to be mostly empty fields. Abandoned structures on the fringe of collapse.

"All right. Okay," I say, sighing. "Enough now."

I'm about to go back to my car when I hear a noise, the sound of a tractor in the distance. I look and far off I can see a man plowing. He does not appear to notice me standing there, so focused is he on his task at hand. I don't move even though I know I should. I'm trespassing, having gone too far down off the highway. There's no reason for me to be here standing alone on a gravel road looking out to nowhere, and whatever reason can't be explained in the brief seconds it would take to get him to hear me. I know the ways in which this story could end. Still, I continue standing there, believing somehow if I don't move maybe he will not see, will eventually turn his plow in another direction.

But he does notice me, and my heart skips as our eyes meet, and I don't know why but I raise my hand. It's instinctual, and it's only after it's up in the air that I quickly recognize my mistake. "I'm sorry, I was just—" I shout, stopping myself before I can finish.

He can't hear me over the noise of the tractor so he shuts off the engine. I watch him stand, and even though I now have the urge to turn away, to get back in my car and go, I wait.

There's a part lodged deep inside of me that believes in this moment's significance, believes if he would just reach out his hand—he may not be the world but he is someone, and his action, however small, feels to me to hold an entire history within it.

I know that the past does not belong to us, that there is nothing we can do with what's already been done, but there is now. Now as I hold my hand in the air, as I look out at this man. Do you see me? Do you finally see? There is just this moment as I stand here with my arm outstretched, my heart full of foolish hope, waiting to see what you will do.

# A Plumb, Falling

A plumb line is made by taking a weight and tying it to a cord. The weight, once suspended, makes a true vertical line. It is a standard to measure what one has built. Plumb lines were once used in construction to make sure that the walls were level. They were used to "plumb" a wall. It is an old tool, one used throughout the world and throughout history. The ancient Egyptians used plumb lines in the construction of their pyramids. The "scales" pictured in hieroglyphs were plumb lines. On each side one can see the weight hung by strings.

In the book of Acts of the Bible, God uses a plumb line. "What do you see?" he asked Amos as he showed him the plumb. For God, justice and righteousness were the plumb line. It was God's scale, this line, measuring the sins we've cast upon one another. In this passage of the Bible, the Israelites have failed to live to God's grace and his law. "I am setting a plumb line among the people. I will spare them no longer," he explained, telling Amos that he would no longer overlook their sins.

Here I am, standing outside in the cold, waiting in line for tickets for the Smithsonian National Museum of African American History and Culture, the only museum dedicated to documenting the life, history, and culture of African Americans. It's only been four months since the museum opened and timed entry passes are completely sold out, but their website says there are a select number of passes held during the week for those who those willing and able to visit later in the day. This morning

I'd called the museum to ask about the likelihood of getting one of these tickets. "Is it worth it to try?" I'd asked the guy who answered the phone. "Or would I just be completely wasting my time?"

"We can't guarantee anything," he told me. "You said it's just you?"

"Yeah, just me. No one else."

"Maybe, you'll get in," he said, "but really there's no telling."

I have flown to D.C. for a conference but I have left it for this, walking the mile through downtown D.C. in search of the museum. I get there an hour before the time the tickets will be passed out and there is already a line. I head to the back of it and wait.

A black couple soon comes and stands behind me in line. Before long, they are talking to the next group of people that have joined us.

"I'm so excited about this I don't know what to do with myself," I hear the woman say.

"We came from New York. What about you?"

"Philly."

"I can't believe it's sold out."

"Yeah, we tried in December and I think when I looked there were tickets and then I checked again and suddenly they were all gone. It's crazy."

Because I keep glancing back, one of them asks me where I'm from. "That's far!" he says when I tell him.

"No kidding," I say, and we both laugh.

The great chain of being, or "ladder of being," was a hierarchical structure believed to have been decreed by God to represent all matter and life. It's a taxonomy formed in a continuous line, a ranking of the natural order of the simplest to the most complex forms. Implicit in the understanding of the great chain of being is the premise that every existing thing in the universe has its own place—God at the top of the chain, followed by angels, then humans, and animals, continuing on. It is meant to be an order of the hierarchy of all existence.

Pseudoscientists of scientific racism drew from the great chain of being for their arguments. If there was an order, a hierarchy, then there were those that were superior and those that were below them.

In 1906, Ota Benga, a Congolese pygmy, was put on display at the Bronx Zoo. He was made to carry around chimpanzees and other apes. For the audience watching, he shot targets with a bow and arrow, wove twine, and wrestled with an orangutan. Eugenicist and zoo director William Hornaday labeled Ota "The Missing Link," believing him to be the last missing link of the evolutionary chain. "Our race, we think, is depressed enough, without exhibiting one of us with the apes," said the Reverend James H. Gordon, superintendent of the Howard Colored Orphan Asylum in Brooklyn. "We think we are worthy of being considered human beings, with souls."

In the United States, scientific racism was part of the justification for slavery. It was easier to commit an atrocity upon someone when one believed that they were lower, or when they believed that they were not even human at all.

It is getting close to time for the museum to hand out the tickets. Like me, others shift from side to side, anxiously waiting for them to start.

An older black woman comes up to the line. "Anyone here on their own? Anyone here alone?" she asks toward the crowd.

"I am," I say immediately. "I'm alone."

"I have a ticket for you then," she says, showing me the printed out paper in her hand. "You can just take this and go right on in."

I stare back at her. She sees my hesitancy and tells me she's a docent at the museum. "I'm not trying to trick you here. I assure you this is a real ticket. All you have to do is take it and go."

"We'll hold your spot in line," the white couple in front of me says. "It's really okay. Go ahead."

I still wait, unsure, too afraid to miss my shot.

"Go," they reiterate, and finally, with nervous steps I step out of line, take the woman's ticket, and go toward the museum's entrance.

The Mason Dixon line was created between 1763 and 1767 when two men, astronomer Charles Mason and surveyor Jeremiah Dixon, set out to settle a border dispute involving the land between the British colonies of

Maryland, Pennsylvania, and Delaware. They constructed a demarcation line among four states, creating the Mason-Dixon line, a cultural border that eventually came to signify the states that permitted slavery versus those that prohibited it.

In order to construct the line, Mason and Dixon lay markers and later cairns through all kinds of terrain and weather conditions. At night, they would take astronomical observations of the stars to guide their way, lying on their backs as they looked through a telescope to measure the angles between the stars and the meridian, the due north line.

Slaves, too, looked to the North Star. Unlike other stars, the North Star always remains in a fixed position, always pointing north. The surrounding cluster of stars creates a picture, what they thought looked like a dipper. They called it the Drinking Gourd, named after the hollowed out gourds used to dip and drink from water. On the cup's edge were two stars that always pointed to the North Star, and in following that line of sight they found the star that would guide their way as they made their passage north of the Mason Dixon to deliverance.

The museum is separated into two sections, the lower three levels detail African American history and the upper floors are of African American culture. Not wanting to wait, the people around me head for the escalators up to see what's there first.

I take the escalator down and am in in a large room where lines are quickly forming. Entrance into the history exhibit has to be spaced out due to the amount of people who've come. I shuffle along with the others to try and find the line's end.

There are rows and rows of people filling up the entire space. They are senior citizens and they are children. They are in wheelchairs and on crutches. They are being pulled along by their parents' arms. As we wait they are sharing their own stories about what they know of the museum, about what it has meant to be black in this country, about Obama's hope. I look at them and I realize that they have been witness to so much of what lies ahead, and yet there is such of collective feeling of joy, of celebration for something long overdue, and standing in the midst of them I am overwhelmed. This will be the moment that gets me, not anything that I would experience later, but this—of being here and being able to share this moment with all of them.

I can feel the ache in my throat beginning, and I have to leave the line before it comes. I find the bathroom, go into the stall, and begin to cry. It takes me a few minutes to get myself together, and when I open the door I see a woman standing by the sink. She looks at me through the mirror's reflection and tries to smile.

"Are you okay?" she asks.

"Yes," I start, my face flushed hot with embarrassment. I'm just—"

"I know, it's a lot," she interrupts, and I realize she believes I've already gone through the exhibit. She takes some tissues from her bag and hands them to me. "Look, we're here, aren't we? Just remember that if it gets too much again. We're here and we're going nowhere."

*We are here*, I think. We have survived because survival has been etched deep within our bones, and after everything that's been done to us we are still here.

There are so many barriers, both imaginary and visible, between ourselves and in our lives. Places we are and aren't allowed to go. The different demarcations of our existence. Our lives, our history, is a compendium of these lines that have been created. For instance, there's the assembly line of slaves—as they marched onto boats, as they marched to be sold, with their bodies on the ships lined side by side, no room to move, no room to breathe.

Or later, in the fields as they worked, their backs toward the sun as they picked cotton and tobacco, chopped sugar stalks.

A stake of wood nailed to another to form a cross, placed in the ground and lit on fire.

Or a rope falling down, perpendicular to the tree from which it hangs.

Eugene Williams was just eighteen years old when he swam south of the invisible line of Lake Michigan's beach, not understanding that the 25th Street beach was for blacks while the 29th Street beach was for whites. When he ventured on the other side of this boundary, whites saw and threw stones. He drowned in the lake, his death a catalyst for five days of race riots that followed.

In our present day, you can draw a single line on the map of certain cities marking the racial divide between whites and blacks. It is Eight Mile Road in Detroit, or Main Street in Buffalo, or Delmar in St. Louis, otherwise known as the Delmar Divide. It is US 275 in Tampa, and US 49 in Shreveport. It is the railroads in Pittsburgh and Hartford. These barriers have been stitched into the fabric of our country, the railroads and highways the thread forever separating us.

We are ushered inside the exhibit, but really what has happened is that we have moved into another smaller room. A guide stands near a glass elevator. He guides a group of thirty in at a time, and once the elevator has descended he begins his speech to the new crowd that's formed.

"Congratulations, this will be the last line you'll have to wait in today."

The crowd laughs in response. The guide then tells us that the history exhibit is over a mile long and that there are no bathrooms until we get to the end. "Go before you start. Make sure you have tissues," he says. "A lot of what you'll be viewing will be difficult, so prepare yourselves."

The elevator comes and I go in with the next group. We pack inside, the doors close, and we go down.

"Look," a child says, pointing, and my eyes follow to what she sees. Now I understand the reason for the glass. As we go down we can look at the walls and see a timeline, counting backward through our history.

"1900, 1800, 1700," we all read out loud, and my heart whispers say her name. As everyone counts my heart aches in the knowledge of the Wilmington riots, of Bloody Sunday, of the bus boycotts and lunch counter sit-ins. I think of prison chain gangs, of poll taxes and literacy tests. Of the cotton is king fields. Of necks broken from the tightening of a noose.

I am thinking of the swing low sweet chariot roads that took us home to freedom. I am thinking of all we risked and all we lost.

*1900, 1800, 1700, 1600, 1500.*

The elevator stops at 1400. The doors open, and what we've waited so long for has now, finally, begun.

My whole life there has been a story I've borne within me and it begins like this—with a child who in the bathtub would scrub her skin raw until it bled while wishing the water wouldn't run so clear, with a mother who also hated herself, who endured an unspeakable pain and died with the secret of it still within her, with a family that harbored decades of shame, with a grandfather whose religion couldn't save him from himself, with a great-grandfather who was light enough to pass, who was forced to pass in order to get to know his father, and lastly with a great-great-grandmother—a woman born in slavery, who became free, and during Reconstruction had a relationship with a white man, a farmer, and who gave birth to several of his children, managing somehow to have one of them carry the father's name so that decades later, over a century, someone, me, would be able to look to this name and know.

I'm told that when this son became older and wanted to see his father, he'd travel the distance to the town where there he passed for white, and no one was the wiser. His identity was categorized in the physical spaces he inhabited. Black in one, white in another. With a literal crossing he shifted identities, how he acted in the world, and what I imagine, what he believed about himself.

The one-drop rule of the time dictated that if you had any black ancestry in you at all, you were black. You could look white, could pass for white, but if it was found that any of your ancestors were black, you were black as well. They came up with other classifications—terms like mulatto, quadroon, octoroon, to describe the sons and daughters who were born looking like their own—but these classifications were meant as further distinctions between what for them was a central distinction. They were not white, something different, something *other.*

So within this prism of understanding, imagine two families. One a white family, another one black. Imagine their children—white children and black children connected by blood with few, if any, racial distinctions between them.

My mother once told me a story of the time they integrated the schools. "They brought all the black students into the auditorium with the white ones, and all the black students went to the back of the bleachers and sat together, and all the white students were in the front, and it was us and it was them," my mother said. "We were here and they were there."

Years after her death I will relay this story to my godmother—my mother's cousin who grew up with her on neighboring family farms. "What makes you bring this up?" she asked.

"I don't know," I said. "It's just been stuck in my mind for some reason. Perhaps with everything in the news."

She pauses for a moment before responding. "I remember that too. After all these years it's really the one thing I also remember—that image of the auditorium waiting for them to call each of us down from our different groups and tell us where we should go. It's funny that between us it's what stuck in both of our minds."

"Why is that do you think?"

"Good question," she said. "You know, it's not that there were so few of us that we grouped together. There was actually a good mix between black and white students at every school, and we were about fifty-fifty, and I don't remember anyone telling us to sit together. By the time I got to the auditorium that's just what it was. So who was the first person? Did someone separate the first group of black students and tell them where to sit? Or did they just sit in the back because that's where they assumed we belonged?"

I could spend hours telling you of the museum—of each one of the displays and what they entailed, of the hours it took traveling up the ramps through the documented centuries. I could describe to you each piece that brought to the forefront the history I have learned and made me see the realities of the stories I'd been told. The cowskin whip lashed on the backs of slaves, or at fragment of rope used to lynched Matthew Williams. The "Colored Only" and "White Only" signs designating segregation. The stool from Woolworth's, Harriet Tubman's shawl, Carlotta LaNier's dress. When I see the Southern Railway Company Car I am able to reach out and put my hand on the exterior.

Before I leave, there is one last line I wait in—a line to go see the Emmett Till exhibit. As I wait, I listen to two students discuss who Emmett was. "Did you hear about how she lied?" one of them says.

"What?"

"It just came out like last week. The woman who said he whistled at her. She lied about it all."

Everyone is quiet once we get to the exhibit, once we're inside the space that holds his casket. I realize too late that I wasn't prepared for this, and so I leave—walking away from the exhibit and toward the exit. I have seen everything by now, and there is no need for me to go back, no need for me to even look back as I find my way out.

I open the glass doors and suddenly I am back where I started, in the main area where I waited with hundreds of others to go in. This feels symbolic, this circling back I've done, but I will not catch this meaning until long after I have left the museum.

They say that progress is cyclical, that it is not a straight, solitary line, despite what we may want to believe, but it instead happens in waves.

What unsettles me when I think of this is to imagine what is coming, because with every moment of progress there comes a moment of backlash. We have made progress and now we are seeing the tide of it recede. So I look at what's come before and I wonder how much will be repeated. I worry that when it comes I will not be ready. I will not be strong enough to weather any of it.

But, I'm told that another way of looking at this is to understand that in order to finally get to some sort of end there must be an examination of the beginning. We must understand the past if there will be any attempt to move forward.

I take this weight and hold it in my hands. I feel its heaviness as the muscles in my fingers relax, letting it slip and fall through the air. If the weight is heavy enough it will sink straight down, but it may not. If it doesn't, I'll watch as it swings. Waiting. Believing that it will steady itself eventually.

And now it ends with this, with me giving thanks—

Thanks to my father who has always supported me and who never once said during all these long years that I should try and do something else.

Thanks to my godmother who made me believe I could, and should, write this story.

Thanks to the women who will never read these words but I must thank them anyway: Leanna Brown, my grandmother, and lastly, my mother. I am sorry for everything you suffered.

Thanks to my childhood friends Cory Fish, Samantha Sowell, and Miracris Calilung. I have never forgotten the support and kindness you showed me when I was younger.

Thanks to my teachers Rick Reiken, Pamela Painter, Maria Flook, and Bill Donoghue. I credit everything I learned about writing from what you taught me at Emerson.

Thanks to my friends Wes Hazard, Hairee Lee, Kimberly Southwick, Alexandria Marzano-Lesnevich, Brooks Sterritt, Peter Desrochers, Joseph Pierandozzi, Olivia Kate Cerrone, Michelle Cronin, Peter Jurmu, Curtis Purdue, Cam Terwilliger, Adam Ahmed, Vince Ugaro, Meg McQuoid, Lillian Kazanis, Erin O'Brien, Renee Algarin. I met you all during my time at Emerson, you were there for me during the death of my mother and for my years of grief after. You believed in my writing long before I did, saw what I couldn't, and I am grateful.

Thanks to Lance Morosini, my first and forever reader.

Thanks to my friends A.A. Balaskovits, Nick Potter, Erin Potter, Scott Garson, Nathan Riggs, Michael Nye, Danny Miller, Jess Miller, Gordon Sauer, Carli Sinclair, Rachel Hanson, Kate McIntyre, Joe Aguilar, Jennifer McCauley, Devin Day, Ryan Habermeyer, Naira Kuzmich, Monica Hand, Tim Love, Steve Haynie, Maria Haynie, Jess Bowers, Evelyn Somers, Dedra Earl, Owen Neace, Maura Lammers, Jordan Durham, Kaulie Lewis. You all supported me during my time at the University of Missouri and through the writing of this book. I have been made better knowing you.

Thanks to Trudy Lewis, Anand Prahlad, and especially Michael Ugarte, who all read an earlier version of the book when it was still just my dissertation with only the dream of being something more.

Thanks to Stevie Devine, Myfanwy Collins, Misha Rai, Rebecca Hazelwood, Silas Hansen, Ploi Pirapokin, Brandon Hobson, Doug Paul Case, Zach Doss, Brandi Wells, Elisa Gabbert, Kyle Minor, Meghan McClure, Meg Meagan, Anthony Michael Morena, Sara Eliza Johnson, Rion Scott, and Nick White. I met most of you online first and some of you I haven't yet met in person at all, and still you have been there for me and I am grateful. When I have felt lost and alone I found you and you cheered me on and lifted me up.

Thanks to Jean Morosini and G.C. Waldrep for your help with any research questions I had.

Thanks to Roxane Gay, whose voice has been the light to me finding my own.

Thanks to Yona Harvey, whose support helped me finish this book when I didn't think I'd be able to continue.

Thanks to my creative writing students at both the University of Missouri and Cornell College. You inspired me every day with your bravery, honesty, and kindness. I am waiting to see what beauty your hearts create.

Thanks to the journals that published pieces from the book: *The Adriot Journal*, *The Los Angeles Review*, *Harpur Palate*, *Indiana Review*, *Passages North*, *Carve Magazine*, *Bennington Review*, *Ninth Letter*, and *Fugue*. Thank you for believing in this project and for sustaining my faith that this work mattered.

Thanks to Diane Goettel, my editor, and the rest of the staff at Black Lawrence Press for your time and effort to usher this book out into the world.

Thanks to the community at Cornell College. The support you've given me during my time at Cornell has been truly life-changing. Thanks also to the families of Robert P. Dana, Stephen Lacey, and Winifred Mayne Van Etten, as well as the other donors for making the Robert P. Dana Fellowship possible.

Thanks to the staff at the Whitney Plantation Museum but most especially to my tour guide Ali, as well as the staff at the Whitney Museum of African American History and Culture, the North Carolina State Archives, the Gunn Memorial Public Library, the University of North Carolina-Chapel Hill Library, and the Family-Search genealogy organization. You all are the true unsung heroes.

Lastly, because representation has mattered in the development of this book and in my own sense of self, I would like to thank Jennifer N. Baker and her Minorities in Publishing podcast, the editors of the journal *Blackberry*, and the following writers for making me feel seen: Morgan Jerkins, Ashley Ford, Samantha Irby, Camille T. Dungy, Khadijah Queen, Danielle Evans, Tiana Clark, Stephanie

Powell Watts, Dionne Irving, Tiphanie Yanique, Jesmyn Ward, Megan Giddings, Dana Johnson, Helen Oyeyemi, Ashley M. Jones, Margo Jefferson, Leesa Cross-Smith, Tia Clark, Safiya Sinclair, Tara Betts, Wendy S. Walters, and Tayari Jones. Thank you for forging the path and for making me feel seen.

—this book I wrote because of you.